A BOY & HIS DREAM

The Art of Crafting a Brand

INDIA • SINGAPORE • MALAYSIA

Notion Press

No.8, 3rd Cross Street
CIT Colony, Mylapore
Chennai, Tamil Nadu – 600004

First Published by Notion Press 2020
Copyright © Khanindra Barman 2020
All Rights Reserved.

ISBN 978-1-63606-932-6

This book has been published with all efforts taken to make the material error-free after the consent of the author. However, the author and the publisher do not assume and hereby disclaim any liability to any party for any loss, damage, or disruption caused by errors or omissions, whether such errors or omissions result from negligence, accident, or any other cause.

While every effort has been made to avoid any mistake or omission, this publication is being sold on the condition and understanding that neither the author nor the publishers or printers would be liable in any manner to any person by reason of any mistake or omission in this publication or for any action taken or omitted to be taken or advice rendered or accepted on the basis of this work. For any defect in printing or binding the publishers will be liable only to replace the defective copy by another copy of this work then available.

Note from the Author

I would like to express my heartfelt gratitude to you, dear reader, for choosing my book.

I was working with one of the best software development companies in the world, and with no expertise in entrepreneurship, one fine day I decided to renounce the corporate world and pursue my dreams of becoming an entrepreneur.

During the early days of my entrepreneurial journey, I had to go through many hardships, not just financially but also in terms of operations. I wished for some help or a mentor, which never came my way. I promised myself that someday I'd dedicate myself to helping entrepreneurs create better brands so they wouldn't have to go it alone like I did.

I tried to share all that I learned during my twenty-two business ventures over the last fifteen years, and to also bring about a profound sense of realization that we need to be good human beings first in order to be successful in life. I hope you'll find the book very helpful for your own journey in creating your dream brand.

I'd like to thank my family, colleagues and all the people who have always encouraged and supported me to share my lessons in the form of this book.

Finally, I dedicate this book to all my readers and those who want to create great and responsible brands to make this world a better place to live.

Love & Peace

Kay

Contents

Chapter 0: There Is No Tomorrow	7
Chapter 1: Meet the Grahams	9
Chapter 2: Another Shot	15
Chapter 3: Morning Has Broken	23
Chapter 4: A New Day	31
Chapter 5: Flamboyance Meets Excellence	39
Chapter 6: The D Day	45
Chapter 7: Don't Expect	53
Chapter 8: A Better Person Every Day	63
Chapter 9: Just Do It	67
Chapter 10: Lobster for Lunch	77
Chapter 11: A Beautiful Mind	81
Chapter 12: The Unexplored Ocean	87
Chapter 13: Stay Close to Nature	99
Chapter 14: The Unforgettable Trip	105
Chapter 15: The Why before the Where	113
Chapter 16: Bonding and Branding	119
Chapter 17: Setup and Infrastructure Planning	135
Chapter 18: Distribution Channels	143
Chapter 19: The Chicken-and-Egg Story	149
Chapter 20: To Socialize or Not to Socialize	155
Chapter 21: Know Everything Inside Out	161

CONTENTS

Chapter 22: Colleagues and Friends	167
Chapter 23: The Preamble	173
Chapter 24: One Collaborates with One and Equals Eleven	179
Chapter 25: The Magic Mantras	191
Chapter 26: United for a Cause	203
Chapter 27: The Promise	207

Chapter 0

There Is No Tomorrow

Is your life meaningful yet?

Gunshots and screams replaced the quiet of an early morning on Ninth Avenue in downtown Naperville, a suburb of Chicago, Illinois. When the cops arrived, they found no one at the scene. Suddenly, an old man, from the balcony of the third floor of a nearby house, pointed the cops toward a boy lying on the ground at the corner of the street. The cops ran to the spot, finding a boy sprawled in a puddle of mud, shot in his right shoulder and right leg just above the knee. Without further ado, they called for help. Within minutes, the ambulance careened around the corner, and the boy was whisked to the emergency department at Edward Hospital on Washington Street.

***

Chapter 1

Meet the Grahams

Every journey is prodigiously beautiful. At the end of it, some realize it was good and some bad. The wise ones learn and the others stay where they are.

John Graham had just turned fifty-two. He'd been born into a middle-class family and devoted his life to keeping his family close and happy. At six one, he had broad shoulders, salt-and-pepper hair, and a big moustache. He also sported a yin-yang tattoo on his right forearm and still had a very athletic body. His destiny had always placed struggles in life, but this never kept him from being optimistic. He believed in savoring every single moment of life and held low expectations for happiness, which was easily achievable, thus keeping him happy and driven.

He was always kind to his friends and loving toward his family, believing in spending as much blissful time with them as possible. He was known to say things like, "The most precious thing I can give my family is time, and I know that every moment spent with them will make wonderful, long-lasting memories. But every moment missed with them is a missed opportunity."

One more remarkable fact about John was that his heart melted for nature, and he would do anything to stay close to it. He loved spending time outside of work absorbed in the arms of Mother Nature, and he treasured the serenity and beauty of his walks in the park.

Having worked in a local departmental store as a stocker for the last seventeen years, John was loved and respected by everybody in the store and well-known as the go-to guy.

He would work late most of the time, as he loved to volunteer to cover the shifts of his colleagues, who would need to leave early. You could often find him sitting in the parking lot with a colleague, listening to their problems and offering his support.

Max, the owner of the store, loved John for his kindness and his relationship with the employees and clients. Max was often heard saying, "John, you need to start taking up managerial jobs at the store."

But John always replied, "You know me, Max. I would love to do that, but I know my limitations, and so I guess I am good where I am. I enjoy my work, but thank you for your encouragement and kind words."

John had only studied through the sixth grade and that made him feel unworthy of a managerial job that would come with lots of complexities. He preferred spending the rest of his working life doing what he was good at and felt confident about.

His wife, Margaret, was equally kind-hearted and loved by her family, friends, colleagues, and neighbors. She was fifty and extremely charming, with shoulder-length hair and an angelic face. Her hair in the front fell beautifully to her eyebrows. She had striking gray eyes and an exceptionally appealing smile. She wore a thin, golden chain with a shiny, black pearl almost hugging her neck. She loved wearing her long dresses, especially the flowery ones. Looking at her, one could judge that she would be a lovely, kind lady.

She used to work as a teacher in a school in the neighborhood. Like John, her most important priority in life was to spend quality time with her family. She always made sure that she had at least two meals with the family, sipped coffee with John in their beautiful little garden, chitchatted, went shopping with her daughter, and mostly irritated her son.

She also loved spending a lot of time helping the neighborhood. Many times, in the evenings, one would find her talking to the young boys and girls, educating them to see the world with a benign eye. She was heard saying, "We should work hard. We should dream big. But don't forget that the most important thing in life is to be a kind and good human being.

There will be a time in your life when you will realize that being successful is not the only goal, but being at peace is more important."

People say that after a few years of marriage, the couple starts looking alike and even starts talking alike. John and Margaret were the perfect example.

They had two children - Asha and Billy. Asha was twenty-three years old, beautiful, and kind. She was five feet nine inches tall, with golden tanned skin. She had soft, blond hair that flowed beautifully to her hips. Her beauty was accentuated by her sharp features. She had dark eyebrows and John's dark-brown eyes. On her, though, they looked deeper and more intense. She loved dressing casually and lounging in her blue jeans, T-shirt, and white tennis shoes. The only makeup she wore was a dark eyeliner, which boosted her casual look. Her simplicity made her look even more striking.

She'd just finished her masters in marketing and was pursuing an internship in a marketing company called Marque.Inc in Chicago. She was extremely creative and an easygoing personality. She was pleasant, caring, and, like the rest of the Grahams, self-contented by nature. She lived a modest life, without many big dreams. Like John and Margaret, she used to be mostly pleased with her life and take things as it comes. She had always wanted to work in a reputable company with a great culture and was very happy when she was selected for an internship at Marque.Inc. She loved her work, the culture of the company, and her colleagues.

At home, she was the heart of the Graham's family. She was softhearted, but tenacious at the same time.

Billy was twenty-one years old, the youngest in the family. He was a frivolous character. He was six three and had an athletic body and arresting features. You could see him and know he spent time at the gym or took part in some form of sport. He had a comb-over, with balding hair on top, and grew out his beard long enough to cover his chiseled jawline. He got his eyes from his mother, a beautiful gray that shone when he was outdoors because it reflected the color of the skies. His skin tone was light brown, and he also flaunted a few tattoos on his shoulder and arms.

Like his parents and sister, he was also generous—but had always failed to pick the right company. Since his childhood, he had easily gotten into trouble, which always made him feel that he was the odd one out in the family. And this belief made him slowly drift away from them.

He'd been a very bright student, formerly one of the smartest in his class. He was stubborn but, at the same time, ambitious. This attitude had made him an achiever in his school days. He'd been extremely focused in whatever he'd wanted to accomplish.

But now, his mind was driven by a hunger to be rich. Being ethical was not a part of his values. All he cared for was to become rich, and that too as quickly as possible, even if he had to take some shortcuts.

He'd never believed in the formal education system and had dropped out of college in the first year. He was of the opinion that he did not have to be part of any traditional education system to be a successful person in life.

He'd also used to be a very affectionate family boy, but with time and company, he'd transformed into a rebel. He'd started spending most of his time with his friends and stayed away from his family as much as he could.

Late nights, underground parties, and occasional drugs were now his new companions. He'd also started helping his friends deliver drugs to people, with an objective to earn some extra bucks. He used to say, "The world is all about money. If you have money, you can do whatever you want."

John and Margaret had tried their best to show him the right path, but they'd failed. He was already out of control and had built a small world for himself with his own perceptions. He was very energetic, and John and Margaret had always wished that his energy levels could have been channeled for the right things. The Grahams had given up on Billy, and they just wished and prayed that, someday, he would realize right from wrong and come back to the old Billy, who was extremely loving, caring, and respectful to his family and towards life.

Billy used to say, "Father, I'm sick of not being able to buy anything that I want to. I'm sick of seeing all my friends have things that I've always wanted. I'm sick of your ideologies. I'm sick of being unhappy all the time."

"Unhappy?" asked John. "I understand you have an irrational drive to be rich. I understand you are blinded at this moment. I understand you feel you are in the wrong house. But, my son, this is the reality—and we need to accept our reality. There's nothing wrong in wanting to be rich in life if you earn it with dignity, not with notoriety. A wrong path will be short-lived. Very soon, you'll realize that it was a big mistake, and maybe then, there's no coming back. It's never too late to do the right thing, Billy."

But John's advice had no effect on Billy, as Billy had already closed himself and made up his own strong opinion about his life. He was a perfect example of a rebel—and a waste of an asset. His frenzied drive to become rich overpowered all his goodness.

***

Chapter 2

Another Shot

The good and the bad are all part of life. They play their roles equally well. Those who learn this early will cherish the good and ignore the bad.

Present, 2:37 AM: John Graham's mobile phone rang, but it was on silent, and so rang unanswered several times as he lay sleeping. Then, the landline rang and rang until Asha came running out of her room and picked it up.

"Hello, we're calling from Edward hospital. Do you know Billy Graham?" said a male voice on the phone.

"Yes, he's my brother," said Asha. "Is everything ok?"

"I'm afraid not," said the man on the phone. "Can I speak to your parents?"

Asha shouted for her dad and mom, and they rushed from their room.

"Dad, it's a call from the hospital, and it's about Billy. He wants to speak to you," said Asha, trembling with fear.

John panicked and grabbed the phone from his daughter. "Hello, this is John. I'm Billy's dad. Is everything okay?"

Margaret and Asha stood nearby, nervous and praying.

The man on the phone said, "Mr. Graham, we're sorry to say that Billy has been shot in his shoulder and knee. The ambulance got him to the emergency room, and from there, we had to take him to the operating room immediately. He's in a very critical condition. Please come over to the hospital, right away."

The Grahams rushed to the hospital and straight to the operating room reception desk, where they asked for Billy.

After some time, the doctor came out and asked the waiting family, "Are you the parents of Billy Graham?"

"Yes, we are," said John, standing up quickly from the waiting room chair. "How is Billy doing?"

"The bullet in the right shoulder seems to be deeply impacted. There's uncontrolled blood loss above the knee, due to injury of the bigger vessels in the limb. We can't say anything at this moment. You would need to complete the formalities of giving your consent before we start the surgery. In the meantime, we're preparing him for the surgery. Please sign the papers at the reception desk, just there," said the doctor, pointing to a nurse waiting with a clipboard.

"Doctor, is Billy going to be all right?" asked Margaret, wringing her hands as her voice trembled with worry.

"We will try our best, and the rest depends on how he fights it out," said the doctor.

"Billy is a strong boy. I'm sure he will win this fight," said John.

After signing the papers, they rushed to see Billy before he was taken away for the surgery. He was lying on the bed with blood all over his body, and he couldn't speak. All they could see were teardrops rolling down his cheeks. Asha and Margaret could not stop crying and kept holding Billy's hands. Margaret almost collapsed. John had to rush next to her and support her. He hugged her and said, "Everything will be ok. Just believe in God, and pray for Billy's life."

They started taking Billy toward the OR. Asha came to John and Margaret, hugged them, and kept crying, upset at seeing her brother in that state. As Billy started moving away from his family, they saw the fear in his eyes. His tears kept rolling down. Deep down, he knew that this was probably the last time he would see his family. There was a sense of repentance for what he had been, and a wish to live again. He could feel the underlying emotional connection with his family, and that made him sob more.

The Grahams were crushed and petrified that they might never see Billy again. Somewhere, deep inside, they were optimistic and hopeful that Billy would fight this out. Margaret broke down completely and needed to sit, to breathe. John and Asha stayed next to her, trying to support each other.

As they entered the OR, Billy started breathing heavily and realized that he was in very critical condition. He felt he was going to die. He could not speak, but a thousand thoughts ran through his mind. *Oh God! What happened to me? How did I get here? How did I mess up so bad? I want to live. Please, God. Please, God.* He was terrified, and he wanted to live. He was pleading to God for one more chance. He'd realized he'd been wrong, and now he wanted to live for his family. The family he'd ignored. He wanted to live for his dad, who he'd never valued, his mom, who he'd never given time to, and for his sister, who he'd never cared about. At this moment, when he was fighting for his life, all he could see around him were things that he could have done, the things he'd never cared to do. He questioned himself—what had he achieved in this life?

He had such a beautiful life, a great family, and he'd wrecked everything. He realized how selfish he had been, that his yearnings blocked out his ability to see anything beyond himself. He was young, and on his deathbed, and there would be nothing that anybody would remember about him when he was gone. His thoughts and realizations kept flowing into his mind while the doctors prepared him for the surgery.

Twenty minutes before the shootout, Billy and his friends had been chilling and drinking at Harry's Bar. It was a Saturday night, and the bar had been crowded. Billy and his friends had been having a great time, but one of his friends, Sean, had looked jittery and was not talking much. Billy came up to him and asked, "Hey, Sean, what's up? Everything ok? You look stressed."

Sean had replied, "It's just a bad day. Otherwise, I'm cool."

Billy had tried to cheer him up and had cracked a joke about how Sean had once been in love with a girl and had never had the courage to tell her. Sean had also laughed, and suddenly, from the right side of Sean, a tall, lean guy had smashed a beer bottle on Sean's head. Sean had started bleeding, the people had started screaming, and in no time, there was a fight between both the groups. Billy knew these were the guys who used to supply drugs to them—and for sure not the kind of guys you would like to get into trouble with. But, at that moment, it had been a matter of survival, and everybody had been just throwing punches in the air.

Suddenly, one of the guys from the other group had taken out a revolver and open fired. Hearing the gunshot, everybody in the bar had started running toward the streets. Billy had been trying to defend Sean, and being a strong guy, had knocked out three guys from the other group. Billy had pulled Sean out of the bar and started running toward the parking lot.

The guy with the gun had come running behind them and shot toward Billy and Sean—and Billy had gone down. He'd shouted, "Run, Sean. Run!" Sean had kept running, vanishing into the streets—and that's when people heard the cops arriving.

Now, Billy's mind was everywhere. A few minutes back, he'd been having a good time with his friends in the bar, and now he was fighting for his life. He had no clue about why the fight had happened. He'd just been trying to help his friend.

Maybe I should have just listened to my parents, thought Billy. *How did I get into this mess? This was all my fault. I started hanging out with the wrong people. I crossed all my lines. I lost all my morals. I never cared for my family. And now, I'm going to die, and there's nothing good that I have done in my life that people will remember me by.* Tears kept rolling down his cheeks. He was scared, remorseful, weak—and, at the same time, he wanted to fight back and live.

I want to live. I want to prove for once that I can be a good human being. I can also... Everything started looking blurry, and Billy found himself going deep into slumber. A dark cloud surrounded him.

The Grahams were waiting outside the OR. Margaret and Asha were inconsolable, and all they wished was for Billy to live. John was shattered but couldn't express himself at that moment. He tried to stay strong and support Asha and Margaret. At the same time, he was trying to be optimistic and hopeful that everything would be fine, and Billy would be well soon. They all kept praying to God, and they waited anxiously for the surgery to be over.

A little more than eight hours later, the operating room door finally opened. All three of them ran to the door and waited for the doctor to come out. After a minute, they saw the chief surgeon coming out. John could see from a distance that the surgeon was walking face down and didn't look happy. This made him panic, and he hoped what he was thinking was wrong.

"Doctor, is everything fine? How is Billy?" asked John, his voice quivering like he was going to break down any minute.

"We managed to save Billy," said the doctor. Everybody let out a huge sigh of relief and smiled. "But I'm sorry to say that we could not save his right leg."

The Grahams went into a state of shock and did not know how to react. Margaret just dropped. She sat down on the floor, not believing her ears. Asha went running to Margaret, sitting next to her on the floor. She hugged Margaret tight and started howling. Tears rolled from John's eyes, and he had no words to express. But, suddenly, he smiled and approached Margaret and Asha on the floor and helped them get up.

He held them both and said, "We are thankful to God that he saved Billy. I know he lost his leg, but we have him. Things could have been worse. This is a moment to be happy for what we have, not cry over what we don't have. Please be strong. Billy won't benefit from seeing us like this." Margaret and Asha tried to control themselves, and they hugged John tightly. They were devastated, crying, but also full of gratitude to have their Billy back.

"Billy is sleeping right now, and he's under observation. He'll be moved to his room in two or three hours, after which he'll be under constant supervision. You can wait for him in his room. Before he comes to his room, I suggest you guys put on a brave face. We have to keep him positive. I'm sure he wouldn't like to see you guys this way," said the doctor. He started to leave.

John grabbed the doctor's hand, thanked him from the bottom of his heart, and said, "Doctor, we can't thank you enough for saving Billy's life. We understand it must have been hard for you, and we're happy that we have our Billy. Thank you, again." The surgeon smiled and slowly walked away toward his office.

They waited for Billy to come to the room. They tried to cheer themselves up so that they could welcome Billy with smiles. Margaret controlled her tears. She realized that she could've even lost her son, but now he was alive. Finally, after two hours, the nurses got Billy to the room, and he was still sleeping. The Grahams waited patiently for Billy to wake up while the doctors and nurses were completing their follow-up rounds.

Billy opened his eyes. Margaret went running to him, held his hand, and said, "Billy, Billy, my son. We're so happy you're okay, my baby." She hugged Billy and cried.

Asha and John also came to Billy's side and smiled. Billy could barely open his eyes, since the effects of anesthesia hadn't worn off yet. But his first thoughts were, *Thank you, Lord. I'm so grateful that you saved me. I pray to you to give me the strength to make my second chance a meaningful life. Give me the strength to make my family proud. Thank you, my Lord. Thank you.* Billy smiled at his family and slowly closed his eyes again. The doctor asked them to let Billy rest.

After few hours, Billy got his full consciousness back. He could feel his whole body in pain and asked, "Nurse, what really happened to me? How am I doing? Am I going to be better soon?"

The nurse replied, "Yes, sir. You'll be fine soon. That's why we're here."

This made him hopeful and put a smile on his face. Suddenly, he realized that he wasn't able to move his right leg. "Nurse, I'm not able to move my right leg. Can you please help me?"

His parents panicked and didn't know what to say—nor did the nurse. She rushed and called the doctor, who came in immediately and spoke very softly and kindly to Billy.

"Billy, when you were brought to the hospital, you had lost a lot of blood. You had bullet wounds in the back of your right shoulder and in your right leg, just above the knee. Fortunately, we could get the bullets out in time and save your life. But—" said the doctor.

"But *what,* doctor?" asked Billy.

"I'm sorry to say that we could not save your right leg," said the doctor.

For a moment, Billy couldn't believe what he'd heard. He didn't want to believe what he'd heard.

"Nurse, can you please remove my blanket? I want to see my leg," requested Billy in a very aggressive and scared tone.

The nurse did so, and Billy saw that his right leg was missing from the knee down.

Tears rolled from his eyes, but he didn't utter a word. The shock was too much to bear. He'd never imagined he would be handicapped, and he didn't want to be. His family broke down and hugged him tight, but Billy said nothing. All he did was lie there, motionless, with his eyes shut, while his family consoled him.

He thought, *why am I living? What now? A second chance like this is no second chance at all.* Nobody knew what he was thinking, and he remained quiet.

John said, "My son, you're a fighter, and we're certain that you will fight this through. We're your family, and we understand how you're feeling. We felt the same way when we found out. We were devastated, but we are also thankful that you're alive. Time will heal everything. You need to stay strong."

Billy showed no emotion and kept his eyes closed, as though in a deep state of meditation. John decided to leave him alone, and the family kept quiet. Margaret sat next to Billy, choking back soft sobs. She held Billy's hand the whole time.

It was one of the darkest days for the Grahams. But, deep inside, they believed that there was a silver lining waiting to be found. They were all optimists, and all they wanted was Billy to recover and have faith in himself.

***

Chapter 3

Morning Has Broken

Family is not just about same blood. They stand by you in good and bad times, accept you the way you are, and make you feel loved without any conditions.

On a Monday evening, after staying in the hospital for nine long days, Billy returned home. Asha and Margaret had decorated the whole house with lights and flowers. They'd also cooked Billy's favorite food. A few neighbors and friends of Billy's came to the house to welcome Billy.

Billy was in a wheelchair and was not too happy—mostly embarrassed—to have so many people see the new him, the *incomplete* him. John quickly realized what his son was going through and made an announcement. "Thank you all for your love, support, and coming over to welcome Billy. I think we should give him some time to himself today. We can all meet on another day." Everybody understood, hugged and wished Billy a speedy recovery, and left.

Billy felt relieved to see everyone leave. He realized how severely he wanted to be alone. However, he'd also become positively conscious that he had to deal with his family. The family who'd never left him alone, even for a single moment, during his bad times. The family who'd cried every moment he'd cried, who waited eagerly for him to smile. The reality moved his heart, and he persuaded himself to be warmhearted toward them. Whatever they were seeking to do, they had only one goal—*to make Billy happy*.

For the happiness of his family, he smiled and asked, "What's for dinner tonight?" Margaret, a highly emotional lady, couldn't hold her tears after hearing these magical words from Billy. But she realized they were tears of joy.

"Asha, let's serve dinner at the table," Margaret shouted with excitement.

They had made some creamy corn soup, salads, cheese, salami, and home-baked breads as starters. They'd also prepared some juicy steaks for the main course. While Margaret and Asha were serving the appetizers, John opened a bottle of wine which he had preserved for nineteen years in his cellar. He poured the wine into four glasses and raised a toast to Billy's homecoming. Everybody smiled, and, for a moment, the family realized how eagerly they'd been waiting for this moment—just to be able to dine together as a family, all four of them. Everybody enjoyed the wine and the lovely dinner, followed by some amazing apple custard and caramel cheesecake.

John and Asha helped Billy to his room and then into his bed. This was new for them, as well.

"Goodnight, Billy. You have a good sleep. If you need any help, at any time, just call me," said John. Then, he left the room.

"Goodnight, my brother. We really missed you at home. We're all so glad to have you back. You go to sleep, and I'll see you in the morning," Asha said softly.

Billy started looking around at all the things in his room, and he felt a different sense of emotion and connection to everything. Earlier, he'd never really seen anything in his room, and today, every small object was magnified and meaningful to him. He could relate to the stories of each and every little thing in his room.

Billy couldn't fall asleep. He was fighting a war with himself. His emotions were tangled. He was feeling depressed as well as thankful at the same time. Suddenly, life seemed blurred to him. Part of him said, *this is the end of my life. I'm handicapped forever and have to always depend on someone. I can never do the things I used to do before. I can never be independent. I can never be equal to my friends. I won't be able do any job, so how will I even survive? Will I be a burden forever on my family?*

These thoughts were destroying him spiritually and pressing him toward obscurity and dejection. A small part of him said, *I have to be tough—if not for myself, for my family. There is a brighter side to these dark days. Maybe things will get better. Maybe the doctor saved my life for a reason. Maybe I can work toward making my life meaningful.* Lost in his thoughts, Billy finally dozed off, exhausted.

It must have been really tough for a healthy, strong young man to suddenly have to accept the bitter fact that he couldn't stand on his legs any more. But John used to say, "Whatever happens in life happens for a good reason. What happened is good. What is happening is good. And what will happen is also good."

The next morning, Asha came to Billy's room and woke him up. "Good morning, brother. I got some coffee for you. And with extra sugar, just the way you love it." Asha smiled.

"Good morning, Asha. Thanks for the coffee," Billy said in a husky, morning voice.

"What do you feel like having for breakfast? Mom and I are going to prepare breakfast for everybody in a bit," said Asha.

"Maybe some cereal and toast? And, yes, some juice as well," said Billy.

Billy continued. "Asha, come here." Asha sat beside him, and, to her disbelief, Billy held her hand and said, "Thank you for everything. I'm not good with expressing my emotions, but, really, thank you. I was the dumbest brother. I never cared for you, and now I feel incomplete without you." Tears rolled down his cheeks.

Asha hugged him. "Don't be crazy and speak rubbish. You've always been my best little brother, and you've always cared for me. And everything will be fine."

Deep inside, Billy knew that she was trying to make him happy. He'd never cared for his family until now. He'd been too occupied with his friends to do that.

"Good morning, Billy," said John, smiling. "Did you sleep well?"

"Yes, Dad! It's really good to be back home in my room," replied Billy.

"Let me help you to the washroom." John helped Billy get fresh.

After a while, everybody met at the breakfast table. Margaret had prepared cereal with yogurt, fresh-cut fruit, and juice, while John had prepared scrambled eggs. They were glad to be together again, chatting about things in the neighborhood, work, cracking up like they used to many years ago, trying to make Billy think about everything else except his health.

"You guys go ahead with your work. I've already taken leave for one more week, so I'll stay with Billy and keep him company." Margaret smiled.

"Mama, I can also stay home if you want some help," suggested Asha.

"No, sweetie. You go ahead. It's your internship, and you need to do well if you want to get a job in the company. You shouldn't be taking more leave," said Margaret.

"That sounds good. Maybe you can give me a list of things you need for the house. I'll get it on my way back home. Anything special you feel like having, Billy?" asked John.

"No, Papa. I'm ok with whatever Mom is preparing. Can you get me a book? It's been quite a long time since I read something," replied Billy.

"Any particular book, Son?" asked John.

"Let me think about it and text you, Papa," said Billy.

John and Asha left for work, Billy went to his room, and Margaret sat to read the newspaper. "Billy, let me know if you need anything. I'm right here in the living room," said Margaret.

"Sure, Mama," replied Billy.

Billy was still getting used to the wheelchair and managed to get himself to his room. He looked out the window into the lush, green garden. He felt his leg with his hand and got lost in his thoughts again.

How will I manage my life?

The same thoughts, over and over again, were eating him from inside. He was losing his faith in life, and he couldn't find any motivation to be alive. His guilt over living a rebellious life, which had led him here, to this situation today, was like a big rock on his shoulders, pressing him down. This guilt of the past and worry for the future was pushing him to gloominess and depression. Billy was lost in his deleterious thoughts. Suddenly, the doorbell rang.

Margaret got the door, finding a young boy of Billy's age standing on the stoop. Since Billy never brought friends home, she wasn't sure who the boy was.

"Hello, Mrs. Graham. My name is Sean, and I'm a friend of Billy's. I'm here to check on how he's doing."

"Please, come in. He's in his room. Let me tell him you're here," said Margaret. "Billy, your friend Sean is here to see you."

The moment Billy heard the name, the scene of the day of the accident flashed in his mind.

"Hello, Billy. How've you been, man?" asked Sean.

"Hey, Sean. Come in, bro. Please, sit," said Billy. "I'm actually not doing so well. The doctors saved my life, but they couldn't save my leg. So, here I am, handicapped for my whole life."

"I'm awfully shaken and shattered. I wanted to come to the hospital and meet you, but couldn't gather the courage. I know all this happened because of me. Brother, please forgive me. I'm really sorry. I never thought that things would turn out this way," said Sean.

"Well, whatever happened is in the past now, and there's no way we can undo it. This is my reality now. I guess this is God's way of making me realize my evil acts," said Billy. "Hope you're out of your mess now."

"The guy who shot you has been arrested and sent to jail. I know that doesn't change the situation, but thought I should let you know," said Sean.

"I don't care, bro. All I care about at this moment is me and my family. Sorry, but I'm not in the right frame of mind," said Billy

"I can understand, Billy. I've also realized that what we were doing wasn't right. I spoke to all our friends about the same. We were so careless that we were ready to throw away our lives for silly things. We want to change, Billy, and we want to change for the better. I know it's never too late to be a good human," said Sean.

He continued. "I know you're in this state because of me, and I can never forgive myself. But I want to let you know that we love you, and we care for you. If there's anything that we can do for you, please let us know. We'll always be there for you.'

Sean stayed over for some time and spoke about their friends. When he was leaving, Billy mustered the courage and said, "Hey, Sean, I really appreciate you coming over to meet me. I understand your feelings and what you're going through. Don't be remorseful for me. I'll be fine. And don't hold yourself responsible for whatever happened. It was never in your hands."

Sean came up to Billy, hugged him tight, and left.

Margaret and Billy had lunch together, after which Billy spent the whole afternoon in his room, wondering and reflecting, looking at the garden and the trees outside. As the day passed, he was completely shattered. The more he thought about things, the more he felt sad for himself. He had no idea how to come out of his hurtful cycle.

"Hey, brother. How was your day?" Asha was back home.

"It was ok. Nothing much, though," replied Billy.

Asha could make out from his reply that her brother was in pain and needed help.

"Hey, Billy, let me just change and come back, and let's have some coffee together," said Asha.

In fifteen minutes, Asha was back with two cups of coffee. "Here you go. This is yours, the one with more sugar. Do you want to sit outside in the garden?"

"No, I guess I'm fine here," said Billy.

"No, it's not fine. Let's go out. Let's get some fresh air, sit on the lawn, and enjoy this cuppa," insisted Asha. She forced Billy to come out with her, and they both sat on the lawn—he in his wheelchair, and she on the garden swing. He was secretly glad she'd gotten him out under the sun. He needed it.

While they were having coffee, Billy was quiet most of the time.

"Billy, it's easy for me to say that I can understand what you're going through. In reality, you'll surely have your own point of view and judgements. But we're your family, and we will always try our best to keep you happy. I just want to let you know that I'm always there whenever you need to speak to me. Today is just the first day, and time will heal everything. I just hope that you'll be free of your pain soon," said Asha.

Asha's words hit Billy hard. He realized how he'd been to his family—and here they were, doing everything possible to cheer him up. He heard Asha, and now he wanted to break down—but he couldn't.

Even Margaret joined them after a while, and they had a great conversation. They sat there for an hour, and then John came back from work and joined them too. Asha got up to get coffee for John, and then they continued. They all felt the great connection they had and how much they'd missed these moments. Billy felt much better and was amazed at the positivity of his family. At this moment, he realized that his family was dedicated to keeping him happy.

***

Chapter 4

A New Day

There will be many deep, dark tunnels in our journey of life. But, at the end of every tunnel, there will be light. All we need to do is fight our way through the tunnel and hope for the light to come soon.

As days passed, Billy went deeper into his shell. He kept to himself. He avoided meeting anybody. He stopped talking to his friends, and he also withdrew from talking to his family. He was fighting with himself, not able to accept reality, and he kept repenting for his past. It was getting hard for his family to see him in this state, and the crier in the family, Margaret, couldn't help but break down, sometimes even crying alone in her room. She tried to take him out in the evenings into the neighborhood, but he only went twice, and then stopped.

John and Margaret realized that Billy needed some professional help. They spoke to him about visiting a psychiatrist, but Billy was not ready for it. He promised them that if he continued to feel the same for one more week, he would do as they said. Asha was the only one with whom he was comfortable talking, but that started shrinking gradually, as well. She realized that she had to do something for her brother—otherwise, they would lose him completely.

The next Sunday morning, Asha planned a family holiday. The plan was to have breakfast at home, go to a nearby orphanage, and then go to the pier for lunch. Billy was in no mood, but Asha forced him to come.

They all finished breakfast and left to We Care, an orphanage in the neighborhood. It was just a five-minute drive from their home. Asha had already booked an appointment with the front desk. There were around seventy children boarding and schooling inside the We Care campus. They entered We Care and met the principal, who was pleased to see them. One of the teachers took them to the kids, and they could see all of them playing, running about in circles, and enjoying the lovely Sunday morning. Asha had gotten a big, eight-pound cake and a lot of fruit for them. The teachers asked the kids to come and meet the Grahams. The kids rushed to meet their new guests and greeted them with affection, smiles, and hugs. Asha made them cut the cake and distributed the cake and fruit.

There were two children with Down syndrome, six physically handicapped children, one blind child, and three deaf-and-mute kids. Billy could see that every child glowed with happiness, and they looked extremely content. They loved the cake and fruit and thanked the Grahams for being so kind.

The kids loved meeting new people, and they were extremely social. They talked and played a lot with the Grahams. Billy spent his time speaking to lot of them. The Grahams could see that Billy was joyful and laughing with the kids. They had been waiting to see Billy smiling for a long time. They stayed there for around three hours, and, finally, it was almost lunch time for the kids. They said bye to all the kids and left from there.

From We Care, they started driving to the pier, which was about forty-five minutes away. While they were in the car, they talked about how charming and positive the kids had been. It had never felt like they were alone in this world or that they weren't family to each other. There had been a reflection of blissfulness on their faces. Billy was quiet most of the time.

They finally reached the pier. Asha had booked a table in a restaurant by the water. They all settled down and ordered some beer and wine.

"How was your experience at We Care, Billy?" asked Asha

"It was nice. The kids were lovely. I guess they have learnt how to be happy in life, which I fail to understand," said Billy.

"Hey, son, there's no comparison here. They're good there, and you're good here. It's all about time and cognizance," said John.

"No, I mean I never expected them to be so happy and positive when they don't have a family, don't have a home, and some of them were even physically handicapped, like me. They have accepted the truth of life and decided to move on and stay happy," added Billy.

"Yes, my son, that's the art of good living. They're not bothered about yesterday; they're not bothered about tomorrow. They just know how to savor the moment. They're not bothered about what they don't have, but are happy with whatever little they do have," said Margaret.

Asha was *wowed* by her mama speaking so brilliantly. Asha has always lived in her shadow and learned the realism of life.

"You see, Billy? You get to learn so much when you spend time with Mama." Asha smiled.

As they sat at the pier, Billy couldn't shake off the morning, or the joy he'd seen on the faces of the kids. As he looked out over the water, he felt a surge of optimism. He saw the birds, the trees, and he felt alive.

They all talked a lot, ate the lip-smacking food, and made fun of Margaret. They came back home late afternoon. It was a great day for Billy. He could see his ray of hope. He could sense the optimism and realized how wrong he'd been.

Before the accident, I always acted like a rebel. And after the accident, I'm acting like a loser. Is this why I asked for a second life? he thought. *I wanted to make this life meaningful, but what am I doing? I'm just lost in my past and scared about my future. Is this really me? I've always been a fighter, and now I'm acting like this is the end of the world. I need to align my thoughts. I'm not the only one-legged person in the world. I've given enough pain to myself and my family, but no more,* thought the new-and-inspired Billy.

It was he who had created this hard shell around himself and pushed himself to depression and sorrow. But for the first time after the accident, he stepped into a new world of optimism. These thoughts got cemented in his mind, and he made a vow to himself that he would work towards a great future.

The following days were much better. A new Billy was born, and he started building a new perspective about life. Billy was filled with gratitude for We Care, which had changed his world. He started going back there regularly. He loved spending time with the kids. Every time he went there, he came back thrilled and filled with positivity. He sat and talked with the kids for hours, played with them, and, many times, even ate with them. The teachers bonded with Billy, and they were glad that he felt happy coming back over and over again to the kids. The kids also established a strong bond with Billy and were thrilled to see him every time.

One evening, Billy and Asha were sitting on their lawn and enjoying their coffee. "Hey, Asha, I would like to thank you for taking me to We Care. To be honest, on the first day, I didn't want to go at all. I went just because I didn't want to play the spoilsport and disappoint the family. You'd already put so much effort into booking everything and getting the family together. But today, I'm so glad I went. Probably, it's one of the best things that happened to me. I'd almost lost hope of living and didn't want to be a burden to my family," said Billy.

"Oh, I'm so glad you loved that place, and it helped you look at life with a new mindset," said Asha, smiling.

"I didn't just enjoy it, but I connected with those kids. There's so much to learn from them and the place. My perception of life has changed, and, for the first time, I believe that I will make the world even more pleasant. This is surely a new life in the real sense, a new beginning—and, I hope, a better end," said Billy.

"Hey, why are you even bothered about the end? That's not in our hands. All we need to worry about is today. I'm so happy to see how your perceptions have changed in the last few weeks," said Asha. "You know, Billy, every situation in life has both good and bad. We are the ones who decide what we want to see—the bad or the good. I'm so glad you started seeing the good."

"So, what's next on your mind, Billy?" asked Asha.

"Well, I don't really know what a handicapped man like me can do," replied Billy

"Can you cut out the self-pity?" Asha said grumpily.

"Ok, I'm sorry. It'll take some time to get over it. You know I'm a newly handicapped person." Billy smiled. "Well, I was thinking that, at some point in my life, maybe I could open something like We Care on my own."

"Really? That's an amazing thought. One We Care of your own, and you can spend as much time as you want every day. It sounds really exciting, Billy," said Asha.

"But, you know, I would need a lot of money to start something like that. So I was also thinking that it should be my *second* venture," said Billy.

"Are you serious, Billy? You have planned everything. I was underestimating you and trying to figure out what you wanted to do. But you have impressed me today." Asha smiled. "So, what's the first venture?" She smiled again.

Billy smiled too. "No clue, Asha. I'll probably surprise you next time as well. As of now, I don't have anything in mind. I always wanted to be rich before my accident, so I guess I have to still live the same dream. The difference is that, before, I wanted to be rich for myself, and now, I want to be rich for others," said Billy.

"Oh, Billy, I'm so happy for you. I'm sure you'll come up with some fantastic business idea for your first venture. I'm always here if you need any help from me," said Asha.

"What's going on here?" Margaret came into the garden.

"Mama, you know Billy has made plans for his future? He has some lovely ideas. He wants to open something like We Care on his own. But he needs money. So he's deciding what to do. He'll become rich first, and then start his dream—a We Care of his own," said Asha happily.

Margaret, as usual, was almost in tears. "No, Mama, not today. You should not cry today," laughed Asha. Even Billy laughed and made fun of his mother for always being so emotional.

"No, I'm not crying. It's just that I'm a little emotional. You guys know that. After all, I am a mom, and all moms have the universal right to be emotional." Margaret smiled. "But I'm so happy to hear Billy's plan. I'm sure he'll do great. After all, he has always been a go-getter and a very intelligent boy."

Margaret could not thank Asha enough in her thoughts for supporting Billy. She remembered how Asha had been named. Just after Margaret and John had married, they'd met an Indian couple who was visiting Chicago, and they'd gotten very friendly. They'd even stayed in Margaret and John's house for a week. During that time, they'd talked a lot about Indian culture and its diversity, which was very fascinating. Margaret and John had gotten to know that there are twenty-two major languages with thirteen scripts and 720 different dialects in India—and a population of 1.3 billion people. They were thrilled to know about the harmony, the diversity, and a lot about the culture and food. They got so inspired by the Indian culture that they'd named their daughter *Asha*, which means *hope* in Sanskrit.

There was happiness in the air, and for the first time in a long time, the Grahams could sense that good times were round the corner. John came back home and joined them. He was absolutely thrilled to hear Billy's plan. He also added his plans of leaving his job and helping Billy in his work.

Billy was very delighted to share his thoughts with his family, who all meant so much to him. He was also very excited that his plan was very well appreciated by his family. His accident had opened his blindfolded eyes and made him realize how important a family was. He also understood how important he was to his family, how much everybody loved him, and the big realization—how much he loved them.

That night, Billy was very excited and couldn't sleep at all. He realized that it would be very tough for him to start something on his own. First of all, he didn't have any money, and neither did his family. Secondly, he had no knowledge or experience about how to start a new business. Thirdly, he started thinking about how he was handicapped, but he quickly brushed that thought away. He believed that his physical state could not make a difference in what he wanted to achieve. He realized that it was going to be tough, and a steep, uphill climb, but he started believing in the power of positive thinking and was sanguine about his success.

***

Chapter 5

Flamboyance Meets Excellence

Every brick is responsible for building a house. Every good deed is responsible for building your destiny.

The next morning, Billy woke up early and waited for Asha in the living room.

Asha came out of her room. "Good morning, Billy. You're up pretty early today."

"Good morning, Asha. Yes, I kind of got up early today. In fact, I was waiting for you to wake up," said Billy.

"Really? When did you start liking me so much?" Asha smiled.

"If you're done pulling my leg, can we speak now?" asked Billy impatiently.

"Ok, ok, calm down. Asha is always at your service." Asha smiled again.

They poured some juice and sat at the breakfast counter of the kitchen.

"You know, Asha, I was up all night thinking about how to get things in place. Then, a frenzied thought came to my mind," said Billy excitedly.

"And what would that crazy thought of yours be?" asked Asha.

"I would need your help. And, please, don't say no," said Billy, building a lot of curiosity for Asha.

"Can you please get to the point?" asked Asha.

"You work with Marque.Inc. I did some research and got to know that your boss is a great mentor. Do you think you can help me meet him?" asked Billy.

Asha was completely surprised, as she hadn't seen this coming.

"My boss? You mean my super boss? Mr. Chris Adams?" asked Asha.

"Yes, Mr. Chris Adams. That's the guy I read about. And I would really appreciate if you could set up a meeting with him," requested Billy.

"Well, he is a very busy man. Also, I'm just an intern. He doesn't even know I exist in his company. I've never spoken to him. But, yes, I can surely speak to my supervisor and try to fix a meeting. But, again, I'm not sure about it," said Asha nervously.

"That would be great," said Billy, smiling.

Asha left for work and all the way she was thinking about how to help Billy to get a meeting with Chris. She was new to the company, and Chris was a very busy man. At the same time, she wanted to help her brother, who was finally trying to get positive in life. She straightaway went to meet Steve, her supervisor at work, and spoke to him about the whole situation. Steve was moved by the story and agreed to help Asha.

"However, Chris is traveling at this moment. I'll speak to him as soon as he's back. If he agrees, then you can get Billy to meet him," said Steve.

"Thank you so much, Steve, for trying to help me out. This means a lot to me," Asha said gratefully.

She got back to her work and texted Billy that she was on the job and would let him know once Chris was back from his travels.

Chris Adams, an exceptionally vibrant personality, was the founder of Marque Inc. It was one of the leading marketing agencies in the country. He was forty-four years old and came with twenty-five years of experience in the industry. Being a very creative person, he'd dropped out of college at the age of nineteen and joined a marketing startup. He then went on to join O&M and worked there for a good nine years. At the age of twenty-nine, he'd decided to work independently and started his own agency, Marque.Inc. It had been fifteen years since he'd started his company, and the clientele included many key brands from different parts of the country, which was why he was frequently traveling.

Chris loved black. He dressed in black all the time. Everything in this room was black. If given a chance, he would make black the brand color of all the brands his agency handled. Whenever he was in town, he spent a lot of time in the office, especially with the creative team.

He was also a very flamboyant public figure. On the weekend, he hung out in the best bars in town. He socialized a lot with the top personalities from the fashion and hospitality industries. He also hosted a lot of private parties for them. He'd never married. He was too busy to think about it. His personal space was always his top priority. But there was also a very soft side to him. He mentored and helped a lot of new entrepreneurs in setting up their companies, and he never charged them for that.

He used to say, "Knowledge means learning, sharing, and learning again." Even though he was busy most of the time, he would still find some "give back" time. His way of giving back was sharing his knowledge and helping young entrepreneurs set up their brands. But one thing was always a scarcity for him—time. So he was very selective in deciding who he wanted to mentor. Billy read about his give-back attitude and was hopeful Chris would consider mentoring him.

Four days later, Chris came back to work. He had been travelling for more than seven days, and the first day back at work was packed. The next day, Steve went up to Chris and spoke about Billy. He explained about the accident, and how he was trying to fight life, and how eagerly he had been waiting to be mentored by Chris.

"Steve, I do mentor young entrepreneurs. But you know I'm very particular about the right person," said Chris. "I have very limited time, and I never waste it on the wrong person. Also, I'm never emotional while making this decision. It purely depends on how good the person is. If I like him, then I will help. Otherwise, I won't."

"I completely understand and respect your opinion. Even they are very well aware of it," said Steve.

"Ok. Please ask him to come and meet me next Tuesday at 9:00 AM," said Chris.

"Thank you very much, Chris," said Steve.

Steve left the room and went straight to Asha.

"Hey, Asha, I've got some good news. Chris has agreed to meet Billy next Tuesday at 9:00 AM."

"Oh, wow! Thank you so much, Steve. I can't tell you how happy this will make Billy. I owe you for this one," gushed Asha.

"But I need to tell you one thing very clearly. Chris is very particular about who he wants to mentor. There are very high chances that he may not mentor Billy. So I want you to prepare him for the same," said Steve.

"Sure, Steve, I understand. And I'll speak to Billy. In fact, Billy knows this very well. Once again, thank you so much." Asha smiled.

Asha was thrilled and couldn't wait to tell Billy about his meeting. She decided not to call him, but instead to tell him in person at home. She couldn't wait to see him.

She reached home a little late that day, at 7:00 PM. John had already reached home by then. As soon as she reached home, she shouted, "Billy, Mom, Dad, please come to the living room." They all rushed to the living room.

"Chris Adams has agreed to meet Billy next Tuesday at 9:00 AM in my office," said Asha with a lot of excitement. Billy was extremely happy to hear this. He understood the value of an appointment with the best in the industry.

"But, Billy, I have to warn you—please don't take this meeting to heart. Chris is a big guy, and he has very limited time. Getting an appointment itself is big. And he's very particular about who he wants to mentor. It's highly possible that he may not even mentor you. So I don't want you to feel bad about it. Just go and enjoy the meeting," said Asha.

"Don't worry, sister. I understand. Thank you so much for getting me this appointment. It wouldn't have been possible without you."

"Don't thank me. Thank my supervisor, Steve. He got the meeting for you. I just asked for his help," said Asha.

It was a good dinner that day, as the Grahams were very happy about the news. They were pleased to see that Billy wanted to turn a new page in his life again. They all prayed that everything went the right way, and Billy could make a new beginning.

***

Chapter 6

The D Day

Opportunities do not knock, but float around us all the time. You just need to have the right eye and mindset to make it yours.

Tuesday morning 8:45 AM, Billy waited at the reception of Marque.Inc for his meeting with Chris. Billy was dressed completely in black. This was his first ever professional meeting, and he had no idea what he was going to present to Chris. But there was a deep sense of assurance that made him feel that this was the day he'd been waiting for. Asha wished him luck and went to her desk.

At 9:10 AM, Laurence, who sat at the front desk, escorted Billy to the conference room. Five minutes later, Chris appeared.

"Hello, you must be Billy. I'm Chris Adams," said Chris. Billy had already seen his pictures on the internet, but Chris looked much swankier than what he had expected. He was around five ten, sharp, and had a salt-and-pepper hairdo, with a neat beard and his long hair gelled and neatly tied up. He was dressed in a black, v-collar T-shirt, black jeans, and a black summer coat that had some tribal-influenced art embroidered in black on the lapels. He was wearing a pair of striking blue shoes and a blue watch.

"Good morning. It's my pleasure to meet you, sir." Billy got up from his chair with the help of his crutches.

"You can call me Chris. Please, be seated and be comfortable," insisted Chris.

"So, Billy, how's it going for you?" asked Chris.

"Well, I would say I'm on the verge of doing something big," replied Billy. "I'm not sure about the past. I don't care about it anymore. I'm working on how to make an outstanding future."

"So, you don't walk anymore. Does that bother you?" Chris had never liked beating around the bush. He was always to the point, which added more to his personality.

"It bothered me a lot, a few weeks ago—to the point that I felt like a burden to my family, like it was useless living. But not anymore. I know now that it was very foolish of me to think like that, and I'm happy that I had my realization quickly. I was newly handicapped and was not able to accept the reality. Now, I don't care anymore, and I feel that I can do what I want to, whether it's on one leg or two. It actually doesn't matter," replied Billy.

While Billy was speaking, Chris noticed something that sparked a curiosity in him. Chris saw that, when Billy spoke about being determined and finding meaning in his life, his eyes would light up.

"Well, you are brave!" remarked Chris.

"Yes, sir, I am now." He chuckled and continued, "I used to be a good-for-nothing. All I did was waste my time and energy with my friends, doing unthinkable things. And then, this accident happened. I've started believing that whatever happens, happens for a cause—a good one. If I wouldn't have lost my leg, I would have probably never realized the value of life. And this realization came to me when I was lying on my deathbed. My life was saved. I am now living for a purpose. And, this time, I'll not let it go. I want to work toward making it meaningful for myself and for the people around me," said Billy with lot of conviction, eyes lit up once again.

Chris was captivated by the positivity of this kid. He had not expected a young boy who had recently lost one leg to be so bold and assertive.

"Do you want some coffee, Billy?" asked Chris.

"Sure, sir, if you don't mind," replied Billy.

"Chris, not *sir*," reminded Chris.

"Sure, Chris." Billy smiled.

Chris ordered two cups of coffee and continued the meeting.

"So, Billy, tell me. How did you overcome these negative emotions? This, uhhh, downside?" asked Chris.

Chris was a smart guy, and he was trying to understand where Billy stood mentally. He knew very well that if someone had to shine in life, it could only happen with a strong and bold mind.

"I was always a go-getter in life. I used to do pretty good at school, but I dropped out in my first year. I didn't like the restricted way of education. I was very focused on becoming rich and got into bad company, which led to bad events. And then, this accident happened. After my accident, I went through a few weeks of trauma. I almost lost hope in life. And then, one day, Asha, my sister, took me to We Care," said Billy.

"We Care? What's that?" asked Chris.

"It's an orphanage near my house. It changed my life. After going there, I realized how wrong I was. Wrong about life, about my attitude, about everything. The kids taught me the biggest lesson of my life—live *now*, in this moment. They were so full of life. They spoke so positively. It was just an incredible eye-opener for me. And, since then, I've started looking at life from a completely new perspective. I believe that I got a new life for a reason, and I will put my last breath into it to making it meaningful," added Billy.

"That sounds interesting." Chris was totally into the conversation.

"Did you go there again?" asked Chris.

"Yes, I did. In fact, many times. Now, I'm a regular there and go there at least three times a week. I feel good whenever I go there," added Billy.

Billy had created a good opening impression about himself. He'd managed to get Chris's complete attention.

"Billy, let me come to the point. What do you want to do now? Why did you want to meet me? And how can I help you?" asked Chris.

"Sure. I'll try to be as clear and short as possible. I want to eventually have my own We Care. But, for that, I need money. So that becomes my temporary goal at this moment. I have to do something to earn money, so that I can use the money to build my orphanage. I want to start working, and I'm sure I don't want to do a job. I'm smart and savvy, and I'm also confident that I can do something big. This time, I just want to channel all my energy into doing something meaningful," said Billy.

"I wanted to meet you because I read about you. I know that you started off with no financial support from your friends or family. I know you're a fighter, and, most importantly, you're grounded. That's why you still help a lot of young people start their companies. I highly appreciate the fact that someone as busy as you can even think about taking out time for young, passionate people who believe in changing the world. I also know that you're very busy and extremely choosy in picking the right person to mentor. And I also had a strong intuition that you would like to mentor me," added Billy.

"And about your last question—how you can help? I'm highly passionate and confident. I have seen death very closely, and I understand the value of life. I understand the value of my family. I understand that my life has to be meaningful. In order to achieve something meaningful, I need a strong cash flow," said Billy.

"So, are you looking for financial help from me?" asked Chris.

"No, not at all. Sorry if I sounded like that. The only help—and the most important help—I need from you is, learn to be a successful entrepreneur. I want to learn the art of making a brand. I want to learn how to build a successful company. I want to learn how to be a successful personality. I know I'm asking a lot from someone as busy as you. But I would highly appreciate if you could help me. I'm ready to commit myself completely to this, and I assure you that I will make you proud someday," said Billy confidently.

"That's quite a long list of things you want from me. Why do you think I should help you? What you're asking for demands a lot of time. I do mentor people, but that's once every few months, whenever I get the chance to meet them, see how they are doing, and guide them. What you're asking for is a huge commitment of time from my end," said Chris.

"Sir, I completely understand your point. I'm looking to learn. I will learn as much as you can teach me. I will be more than happy with whatever you're willing to teach me, whatever your schedule allows. I'm also ready to make myself available any time, on any day convenient to you. If you feel that I have the zeal to be a successful entrepreneur, then I would be more than happy to be your student. Please don't look at me as a handicapped person like many do," said Billy.

"Absolutely not. I would not have spent two hours with you if I had that thought in my mind," replied Chris. "You did a great job in pitching yourself. But I'm sorry to say that I won't be able to take this up. I have to be honest. You're good, and I also feel that you can do great things. But I'm the wrong person. I'm sorry, Billy. We'll be in touch," said Chris.

"I respect your time and will do the same in the future also. I believe that I can do well, and all I need is a mentor like you, who can show me the light. I'd wish that you reconsider your decision," requested Billy.

"Sorry, Billy, I always like to get straight to the point," said Chris.

Billy was quiet for some time. He'd felt everything had been going so well, and suddenly, lightning had struck. But he smiled and said, "I would've loved to have been mentored by you. But I guess you have your reasons. It was really nice to meet you, Chris," said Billy. He started getting up from his chair, making an effort and trying his best to move out of the chair and use his crutches to leave the room.

"So, what's your plan now?" asked Chris.

"Honestly, you were my first plan, and I was very positive that you would work with the reformed me. But I completely understand your tight schedule, and it's fine. Fact is that I'm very clear about my goals, and there's no going back. I have learned it the hard way, and, this time, it's not going to change. I just need to find a way to reach my goals. I'm very optimistic that I'll find my way very soon. I will surely be in touch and keep you updated," said Billy. He started leaving the conference room.

"Wait," said Chris. "I've met many people, but never have I met someone as confident and clear as you. You're tough on your goals, and I'm impressed."

Billy stopped. He couldn't understand what was happening. It had been Chris's way of finding out how tough Billy really was.

"Sorry, Billy, the last part was to double-check that you were strong about your goals. You've convinced me about your passion. I would love to mentor you. You have to give me a day's time so that I can check my schedule with my secretary and see if there's any possibility of us working together. She'll call you tomorrow. Sounds good to you?" asked Chris. Billy couldn't believe that Chris had actually been testing him.

"Absolutely, sir! I'm glad to hear that. I'll eagerly wait to hear from your office. Once again, reiterating, I'll never leave any stone unturned to make you proud," said Billy with a firm voice and mind.

"It was lovely meeting you, young man. I wish you all the best in your life, either way. Take care." Chris started to leave the room.

He suddenly came back and asked, "Was this all black outfit intentional, or is it something you like?"

"Sir, I read about you and saw your photos. You love black, and this was just a small effort to be like you," replied Billy.

Chris smiled and said, "Let me tell you one more important thing. Good is never enough, and you need to be at your best. You were at your best today, and I liked that."

Chris left the conference room, and Billy kept gazing at him as he slowly walked away.

Asha was anxiously waiting for the meeting to get over. As soon as it did, she rushed to the conference room to meet Billy.

"How did it go?" asked Asha.

"I guess I did good. Sorry, I did my *best*," Billy corrected himself. "But I'm not sure yet. He's a very busy man. He's asked me to wait until tomorrow, and his secretary will call me and let me know if he can make enough time to mentor me. So, I don't really know," said Billy.

"Don't worry, Billy. You did your best. We'll see what he has to say tomorrow. Just be positive about it and happy that you had a great meeting," said Asha, smiling.

Billy came home and told Margaret about his day. She, being very positive, felt that Billy had done well, and things would surely go his way.

It was one of the longest nights ever for Billy. He would surely remember this day for the rest of his life.

***

Chapter 7

Don't Expect

The longest—or the best—of journeys start from zero. It's your fury and grit that decide your destination.

Billy was very excited and got up early the next morning. He was restless and couldn't sleep well the entire night. Early in the morning, he went out of the house and enjoyed his coffee on the lawn, watching people out for their morning jogs and strolls. There were mixed feelings of euphoria and anxiety inside him, which made him think, *What an amazing morning it is today.* He could feel the fresh morning air. He could smell the aroma of the white lilies. He could hear the birds chirping. He could see people smiling. There was something very special about this morning. Billy realized that it was actually the situation around him that made the moment special.

At 11:39 AM, Billy's phone rang. His heart started thumping with nervousness. He picked up the call. "Hello, Billy here."

"Hi, this is Emilia, calling from Chris Adam's office."

"Hey, Emilia. Been eagerly waiting for your call. I hope you've got good news for me." Billy smiled.

"Well, Billy, you have to decide whether it's good or not. Chris has agreed to meet you for the first session, and then take things forward from there. Honestly, he's not sure about the amount of time you would need, and so he wants to be double sure after the first session. He wants to meet you next week, Thursday at 8:00 PM, at his penthouse. I'll send you his location and house details. Can I confirm the date and time with him?" asked Emilia. There was too much information too soon for Billy to process, but he knew what he was going to say.

"Yes, absolutely. I'm completely free. I can come anytime, as committed," said Billy with a lot of enthusiasm.

"Is this good news?" Emilia smiled.

"Yes, yes. It's brilliant news. Thank you so much, Emilia," replied Billy.

Billy was very excited to hear this. He didn't bother about the fact that it was a trial session, and Chris would decide based on the first session. He thought that this was just the beginning, and things would get better. He immediately called Asha and told her what had just happened. She was equally excited and wished Billy the best. Billy thanked her, and she replied that what he'd get was everything that he deserved. All she'd done was try to get the meeting set up and everything else had been achieved by Billy himself. She predicted that this was the beginning of happiness for her brother.

Billy had been reading and researching a lot about entrepreneurship, brand building, success stories of bigger brands, and more. He'd also researched about brands launched by Marque.Inc. He wanted to understand the do's and don'ts of Chris's style of working. This was not to impress him, but Billy honestly felt and liked Chris and the way he worked. Billy could relate to it and wanted his own work to be on the similar lines.

Thursday evening at 7:45 PM, Billy reached the reception of the apartment. He had hired a taxi from the neighborhood to drive him, as he was not sure what time he would come back. He was carrying a brand-new notepad which he'd specially bought for this occasion. He waited, and at 8:00 PM sharp, requested the person at the front desk check on Chris and inform him that Billy had arrived.

The front desk executive showed Billy the way to the elevator. Billy got inside the elevator and pressed the twenty-ninth button. The elevator opened to a big, open space, and there were three doors on the same floor, all to three different houses. Billy went up to Chris's house and rang the bell, and a pleasant-looking gentleman opened the door for him. He was dressed in a black suit over a black shirt, with sparkling black shoes.

"Hello, my name is Smith, and I am the butler of the house. You must be Mr. Billy?"

"Yes, I am. I'm here to meet Mr. Adams. I have an appointment with him at 8:00 PM," said Billy.

"Yes, sir, he's waiting for you in the terrace, by the pool. I will show you the way up," said Smith.

Billy entered the house and was mesmerized by the aura of it. It was a penthouse on the twenty-ninth floor, facing the pier. Once you entered into the foyer, it opened up into a double-height living room, probably thirty by fifty feet. There was a big chandelier at the center of the living room, made from black metal, with an abstract, minimalistic design. The sofas were low, contemporary, and had matte gray fabric. The coffee table and the dining table looked like they were made from refurbished wood, with a raw, matte finish. The living room connected to a colossal balcony, separated by plain glass and overlooking the pier. The light-gray, shimmering, sheer fabric was moving about with the gentle breeze from the balcony, like it was swaying to music. The lighting was indirect and dim, creating the perfect relaxed setting. Toward the left of the living room, there was a massive island kitchen made in pure-white, super-matte finish. The island part of the kitchen had a rustic, wooden breakfast counter and looked like the perfect place to socialize. The color palette of the house was black, gray, and white, with small touches of wood to make it warm, and the design tone was minimalistic, with straight lines. Once you got near the kitchen, you could see that there was one more door in the living room, probably leading to a room. Next to the kitchen was an all-glass elevator going to the next floor. The elevator was like a savior for Billy, as he could easily take his wheelchair inside and reach the next level. As soon as he got out of the elevator on the next floor, it opened up to a smaller living space. The living space connected to a lovely, open, wooden deck terrace with a beautiful garden and a medium-sized swimming pool. Next to the swimming pool was a nice-looking glass bar, where Chris, looking dapper, was sipping his drink, listening to some sixties soul and funk music.

He was in his customary black jeans, black shirt, and comfortable-looking red shoes. He was also wearing a red-colored watch to match his shoes.

"Hello, Chris, very good evening." Billy rolled near Chris.

"Hey, Billy. How have you been? Welcome to my house," said Chris.

"Thank you, Chris, for giving me the opportunity to meet you for this session. I feel highly privileged," said Billy.

"Oh, don't worry, you deserve it," said Chris.

"I must say, you have a dream house. It's so well done, and I'm so in love with the minimalistic design approach. It's spacious, the air dynamics are great, it's stylish. Well, I could go on and on," complimented Billy.

"Well, thank you, Billy. Ironically, I don't use the house much. I just enjoy this terrace space, which helps me rejuvenate after a hard day's work. And Smith has always been great help and company," added Chris.

"So, what can I offer you to drink?" asked Chris.

"I will go for a cola with some slices of lime and ice," replied Billy.

"You can ask for any drink you want. I have a good collection from around the world," said Chris.

"Not right now, sir. I'd prefer not to drink when I'm working, especially when I'm learning," smiled Billy.

"Oh, come on, it's fine. You're not really working now. You can have a drink if you want to," insisted Chris.

"I'll have a cola for the time being, and let's see how the evening goes. I might upgrade in a while," Billy said with a smile.

"So, where do you want to start, Billy?" asked Chris.

Billy took out his notebook and pencil exactly the same way someone would before the start of a class. "I'm not sure where to start, Chris. I'm a blank book, waiting to be written in. I'll try to follow your guidance and teachings. I might have more clarity, and probably many questions, as we proceed with our discussion," said Billy.

"You said you want to eventually do something like We Care, but before that, you want to start your own business and make some money," recapped Chris. "I suppose you don't have any funds at this moment, nor do you have any experience as an entrepreneur."

"No, sir, not at this moment. And that's what I want to learn from you." Billy added nervously.

"I guess I have to start from scratch," said Chris.

"Yes, sir, I guess so," said Billy.

Chris asked Smith to refill his drink.

He loved Scotch on the rocks with a slice of lime. He also kept a glass of water next to his drink every time. This was to ensure that he was well hydrated, and he made it a point to have one glass of water after one glass of his drink.

"Well, Billy, since we have nowhere to start from, I would say we can start anywhere, which is good in a great way," joked Chris.

Billy was unexpectedly impressed to see that Chris actually considered such a crummy situation to be positive. He'd almost had an anxiety attack, assuming that this was going to be the end of his evening, and he would be asked to go back right away. One big lesson he could take away from this situation was that, at any point of time in our lives, we could either pick the good or the bad. It all depended on how we chose to see things. Positive people saw only the good, and negative people mostly saw the bad.

"Let me start about by introducing myself. It's always good to know each other better before working together," said Chris.

"That would be really nice," said Billy excitedly.

"Well, I come from a similar financial background to yours; my parents were always struggling to make ends meet. They somehow managed to support us so we could grow up to be positive and kind human beings. At this point in my life, I would say that they did amazingly well with their children. They couldn't afford to give us a luxurious lifestyle, but they made us qualified enough to earn our own luxury. They never compromised on family time, they never compromised on values or on education," said Chris in a deep tone.

He kept sipping on his drink. Meanwhile, Smith checked on Billy to see if he would like to order some appetizers or a drink. Billy was feeling hungry, since he didn't find time for dinner. So he ordered a chicken teppanyaki and a repeat of his cola along with the appetizer.

"I dropped out of college when I was nineteen," continued Chris. "Somehow, I couldn't relate to academics. There was so much knowledge available outside college that had no boundaries, no set patterns, no defined rules, that I decided to drop out of college. I see that you're a college dropout as well," said Chris.

"Yes, Chris. I couldn't relate to it, either. I was driven by an absurd dream to become rich. My intentions changed after the accident, but the dream remains the same. Before my accident, I wanted to be rich for myself, which was a selfish goal. Today, I want to be rich to have a more meaningful life, where I can contribute to humanity," replied Billy.

"Well, Billy, let me ask you one question here before I continue with my life story. There is nothing wrong with being rich for yourself. Why did you change your intent?" asked Chris.

"Sir, this life of mine is a gifted life. I had two bullets in my body, and the doctors had almost given up. But they somehow managed to save me. They said it was a miracle. I lost my leg, but I got a second life. And in this life, I don't want to be selfish. I want it to be more meaningful. I want to die with a smile on my face. I want to die with the satisfaction that I did good. I know I'm too young to speak like this, but one death has made me see many decades." Billy smiled.

"Quite a story you have," said Chris.

Smith got the appetizers for both Chris and Billy and served them on the table. He also refilled both the drinks and went back to the bar. He realized that the gentlemen were in the middle of an intense conversation.

"So, where was I?" asked Chris.

"You dropped out of college," reminded Billy.

"Right. So, I dropped out of college and started painting walls, murals mostly. Many people liked my work and started giving me small odd jobs, like painting the wall of a café, painting offices, sometimes even small walls of homes, and I started making money for my survival. My first employer, Richie, happened to visit one of the cafés where I had painted all their walls as per their theme. He saw the depth in my work and asked the owner of the café for my number. And, after about five minutes, Richie called me up, and all I remember is that the next morning at 9:00 AM, I was at his office. He had more than twenty years of experience in the marketing industry and had just launched his new agency. He hired me as a graphic designer. I was good at my designs, but not a pro at putting them into the computer. But, slowly, I learned the digital part, and I started doing very well. I was appreciated for my work by Richie, as well as many of our clients at that time," said Chris.

Billy kept listening very intensely, and his eyes expressed how involved he was in the discussion.

"Richie was a very creative guy, but maybe not a great businessman. Many times, in our industry, people are eminently creative, but lack the sense of business, which makes their agencies fail. The same happened to Richie. He was striving to pay our salaries on time, and finally, after a year, he decided to close the agency and get back to a regular job. He referred me to one of his friends at O&M, and I got hired. That's where I had my biggest education. I worked there for nine long years with the best brands across the globe. It was an exceptional exposure for me to understand the life cycle of a brand. I would have launched more than fifty brands in those nine years," added Chris.

"I'm a loyal person and don't believe in jumping jobs. I realized at the end of my nine years at O&M that I was in a much better position than any of my colleagues who'd switched jobs. I became the creative director at O&M at the age of twenty-five. After that, I handled many big brands and finally parted after nine long years. It was hard for me to believe that I was actually launching my own agency. By then, I had learned the art of business, as I was involved in managing and launching many big brands. And it was time to practice the same for my own agency. And on February 11, 2005, I launched Marque.Inc," said Chris.

It was already 10:35 PM, and Chris got up from his seat and went to the washroom. Billy pulled himself near the glass railings, from where he could see the whole city, dazzling beautifully, decked up in lights, and also the calm pier. He could feel the soothing breeze from the lake gently hitting his face. He was extremely delighted to be there, talking and listening to Chris.

After hearing Chris's story, Billy's respect for him shot up. What was written about Chris on the internet was very different from who he actually was. He was a much better person in reality. The internet appreciated him as a great marketing guru, but never spoke about his personal life and achievements, which Billy realized then.

"Billy, you need to pour a drink now. This, to me, is two friends talking, and I would be happy if you'd have a drink and join me," said Chris.

"Sure," accepted Billy, and he ordered a gin and tonic with a dash of lime and a lemon wedge on the rim. He also requested the drink to be served in a wineglass.

Smith got the drink in a jiffy, and it came in the biggest possible wineglass. "Why gin and tonic in a wineglass?" asked Chris, finding it difficult to comprehend.

"Just for feels, sir," Billy said.

"Feels? Nice." Chris smiled, still wrapping his head around changing times and generations.

Like two buddies hanging out at the local bar after a long day at work, they clinked their glasses, said cheers, and sipped their drinks. Chris was already on his fourth drink, and he was in no hurry to wind up. They continued their conversation.

"So, how was it starting your own agency?" asked Billy.

"It was nice. A lot of fun. I would say the first year was extremely difficult. However, we stood strong together and worked toward our vision. And now, we're here today, doing quite well," said Chris.

"Sir, you're being modest. Your agency is one of the best in the country, and I must say, you deserve it," said Billy.

"For me, success is not about how much money we're making. It's about the culture in my agency. It's about how happy my colleagues are. It's about how they feel like a part of the agency," said Chris with a lot of pride.

Chris asked for a repeat of his drink. He also got a refill for Billy, but Billy very humbly declined and stuck to his first drink.

"That was about me," said Chris.

"That was very inspiring, sir. I hope someday I'll also be able to tell my story the same way you did, to someone who has a big dream like mine—the way I dream of being like you," said Billy.

"It's good to know that you have your dream. Sir Albert Einstein said. 'Imagination is everything. It's the preview of life's coming attractions.' So, keep dreaming," added Chris.

"I know you don't have any money to invest right now. I know that you don't have any experience, but there is something I see in you that makes me want to help you. I have been working and helping many people, and one thing that I learned very early on, and very well, was to understand and perceive successful people. And I firmly feel that you can be a successful entrepreneur. So, yes, I will mentor you on how to build a brand, how to be successful," said Chris with lot of confidence.

"Sir, I am extremely overwhelmed and happy to hear that from you. This is my first dream come true, and I'm sure there are many more to follow, if you are there to mentor me. I will surely give my heart and soul to this. I will put in my all and make you proud," said Billy with conviction. He was glad to realize that it was finally official.

It was midnight already, and Chris was working the next day. So they decided to call it a night. Chris told Billy that Emelia would get back to him about the next meeting's time and venue.

Billy bid adieu and called for the driver, who was waiting in the parking area. On his way back home, he felt highly accomplished and prayed to God to give him the power and strength to live up to Chris's expectations. He had no direction at that moment, but had faith that, soon, he would find out what he wanted to do in life. With a lot of determination and positivity, he snuck into his room and went to bed. It had been a highly satisfying day for him.

***

Chapter 8

A Better Person Every Day

Revenge and ego are two heavy weights on one's mind. Forgive, and relieve oneself.

That night, Billy slept very well. The next day, he got up and met everybody at the breakfast table with a broad smile and enthusiasm, and he briefed them about the previous night. The Grahams were extremely happy to see Billy making his dream a reality independently. They were also hopeful that one day Billy would do well. They loved the new Billy, who had transformed into a great soul with a bigger purpose.

Billy wanted to work on this positive approach of his and fill his life with good habits. He was highly inspired by the book *Atomic Habits* by James Clear, where it stated that we should adapt at least one good habit or give up one bad habit every day. The results wouldn't show immediately, but if we continue practicing, the results in the long run would be compounding. He wanted to practically live his learnings and be a better person every single day of his life.

He bought a nice-looking journal. He started writing down every little thing he wanted to improve in his life. He realized that it was not easy to acquire new good habits and abandon old bad habits. So, this journal was his key to measure his success. He defined all his personal as well as professional goals. He was true to his journal, and whenever he looked back, he realized that he had actually started doing better every single day. He always carried the journal with him and wrote whenever he got a new idea. He read the journal at least twice a day—morning, as soon as he would wake up, and at night just before going to bed. Billy started waking up early and would finish his training and meditation. He progressively traveled into a life of thinking good, talking good, feeling good, and doing good.

One afternoon, Billy was looking out his window, and, without any warning, a strong realization hit him. All this while, somewhere in his mind, he'd had the feeling that his accident had happened because of his friends, mainly Sean. But now, he realized that *you reap what you sow*. Had he been clean, he wouldn't have landed in that situation. It was not just his friends who'd been involved with the wrong people, but he had been, as well.

He also read in one of his books that any unsettled feeling of resentment, vengeance, or ego was a self-crafted burden that you have to carry as a load on yourself. So, he became conscious that he should forgive his friends and relieve himself from these thoughts.

Billy called Sean. "Hey, Sean, what's up, brother?"

Sean was flabbergasted to get a call from Billy, as they'd not spoken since the day Sean had come to visit Billy at his house.

"I'm doing good, Billy. How have you been?" asked Sean.

"I'm doing well. Coping with this new life, and it's not as bad as I guessed it would be," replied Billy. "Are you guys still meeting up at Harry's every weekend?" asked Billy.

"Yeah. In fact, we're all catching up tonight at Harry's. Would you like to join us?" asked Sean.

"Yes. I was actually thinking of coming and meeting everybody. It's been quite a while since I hung out with you guys," said Billy.

"Wonderful! Everybody would be so glad to see you. See you there, brother. Tonight at eight," said Sean.

During the day, Billy spent most of his time reading, listening to podcasts, watching TED Talks, and researching on the internet. Every single day had been a huge lesson for him. Life had steadily become more exciting for him, and he'd started looking forward to the next day.

Billy finished his dinner with his family, and at 7:30 PM, he headed to Harry's bar. His family was a little tense because he was meeting the same people at the same old place.

Before leaving the house, he assured his parents that he wouldn't do a late night and would be back by 10:00 PM. He reached Harry's on time, and he could see his friends sitting in their regular table by the window. He went up to the table, and they helped him get settled into a chair. Everybody was extremely delighted to see Billy.

"Hey, Billy, so glad to see you, brother," said Sean.

"Yup, it's great to be back here," replied Billy.

Billy ordered his regular beer. The bar owner and the manager came up to Billy to check on him and how his health had been. It'd been more than four months since they'd seen him, since the day of the accident. Billy couldn't believe that this was the same place where his life had changed. Nevertheless, it was nostalgic to be back.

Billy was the center of attention, and everybody was trying to check on him and find out how he was doing and what was going on his life. They were all old friends and always wished the best for Billy. He realized that he should have met them long ago. But it was never too late, and he was glad that he'd come over. All his friends were amazed to see the super-positive side of Billy, and it was beginning to inspire them.

"Hey, guys, I wanted to speak to you about something important," said Billy.

Everybody turned to Billy and waited for him to speak.

"I know whatever happened last time was very unfortunate. I would like to tell you all—and especially Sean—to please not consider yourself responsible for the accident. It was destiny and it had to happen. I understand that none of us would want this to happen to any of our friends. I don't want any of you feeling guilty about it. To be honest, in the beginning, I also felt that I was handicapped for life, for no fault of mine. But that's not true. I was a part of everything. I was equally at fault, and it was purely because of how I was in the past. So what happened to me was purely because of me—and nobody else," said Billy.

Tears rolled from Sean's eyes, and he hugged Billy and said, "Brother, I can't thank you enough. I've been unable to have a moment of peace because of all this guilt. I can't sleep at night, and I always wish that what happened to you had happened to me. You were just helping me, and the whole mess was because of me. And today you have shown how big of a heart you have and how kind you are. Thank you, again."

Everyone got emotional and smiled to see both of them back together, and they tossed up a drink for Billy. "Here's to a bright future! Here's to Billy," shouted everybody.

Billy continued. "I've been through a lot of pain, but I've steadily started perceiving the true meaning of life. It's about being responsible. It's about being kind. It's about being true. I would personally suggest that all of you have a lot of fun in life, but please keep yourself away from anything that's evil. If you don't, it will eventually come back to get you, and by then, it might be too late for you to retreat." Billy's words pierced into the hearts and brains of his friends, and they were still for a moment. The rest of the evening, they had lot of fun talking and rejoicing, reliving old memories.

It was 10:00 PM, and Billy said bye to all his friends and promised to meet up again soon. He also asked them to come home anytime if they wanted to meet him. They were all delighted that Billy had come. On his way back home, Billy felt extremely light and relieved that he'd forgiven Sean and eased Sean's guilt. Billy felt as if he had been carrying a huge and heavy stone on his shoulders, and today, it was suddenly gone. He smiled to himself and thought about his journal. His good deed for the day.

He reached home and opened his journal. He was happy to see that he could put a tick on a very important point—forgive one, forgive all.

***

Chapter 9

Just Do It

Plant a tree. Don't worry about the fruit. Just take good care of the tree every day. The fruit will surely be the best.

Monday morning, Billy got a call from Chris's office. Emilia asked Billy to meet Chris on Saturday morning at 10:00 AM at Millennium Park.

"Chris goes there for his run every Saturday at 9:00 AM, and he would like to meet you after his run. Can I confirm the same?" asked Emilia.

"Yes, please," Billy replied instantly.

Saturday morning, Billy finished breakfast with his family and headed out to Millennium Park. Asha was going to downtown Chicago herself, so she gave Billy a lift.

At 9:50 AM, Asha dropped Billy off. "You take your time. I will be with my friends. Call me once you're done, and I will come and get you." Billy was glad that he got a free drop off and pickup.

"Hey, champ, how're you doing?" Chris came running up from behind Billy and surprised him.

"Hey, Chris. I've been doing good, very well, indeed," replied Billy.

"Oh! You sound great. Let's grab a seat somewhere," said Chris.

They found a nice little isolated area in the park with two benches. Billy preferred sitting on his wheelchair.

"See, this is one of the advantages of being in a wheelchair. You don't really have to search for a seat," joked Billy.

"True. I can see that you've started searching for the good things in life. I can see that you're seeing the positive now. I'm happy for you, Billy," said Chris.

Chris sat on the bench and was doing his regular post-run stretches. Smith came up behind him with a fruit basket and some juice. Smith arranged a small table in front of Chris and laid out the fruit, juice and some water.

"Sir, I'll be taking a small walk or sitting nearby. Please give me a call if you need anything, and I will be right here," said Smith before he left for a little stroll.

"Please, pick whatever you feel like eating or drinking," said Chris to Billy.

Chris took an apple and a bottle of juice and asked Billy, "Tell me what you did last week. What made you feel so good?"

"I met my friend Sean—and other friends as well—over a drink. All this while, a part of my mind always thought that whatever happened to me had been because of Sean and a few of my friends. I realized that I was wrong, and I should speak to them about it. So, I met them and convinced them not to feel guilty about my accident, and that none of them were responsible for it. I got to know that they'd been actually feeling guilty all along, and Sean was extremely upset. When I spoke to them, they were so relieved and happy to hear from me. It was a great emotional moment for all of us, and we are now back together," replied Billy.

"Oh, so good to hear you did that. You must be proud of yourself," said Chris, and their conversation started.

"Yeah. Besides that, I've been doing a lot of meditation and positive reading and trying to practically live my learnings each day," said Billy.

"Okay, great. So now, back to business. Since we don't have a business model in place that can help us start our discussion, I'll start our learning from the very basics of how to create a successful brand," said Chris.

"Sure, Chris, that would be great," added Billy excitedly, his eyes all lit up.

Billy opened his notebook. He was all geared to write down each point mentioned by Chris. He also put his phone on flight mode and started recording the conversation. Billy intended to go back and listen to the conversations over and over again to have a better understanding and make detailed notes.

"What is your understanding about a brand?" asked Chris.

Billy thought for a while and replied, "I would say a brand is the name and identity of a single—or more than one—product from a company."

"Technically, you're right, Billy," said Chris. "But when it comes to creating a brand, it's much more than just a name or a symbol," added Chris. He continued, "A brand is a promise, a story, a perception, a belief, and an established sense of trust. All these factors combine together to create an exclusive identity. That's the brand."

"It's a brand that allows you to build loyal customers. It's a brand that gives confidence when it comes to the quality. It's a brand that allows you to have a higher price for the same product. It's a brand that reminds the customer of your promise. It's the brand that reassures the customer that they can trust this promise," continued Chris.

"And, internally, the brand values contribute towards creating the right culture for your company. Hand in hand, the brand and its culture attract the right people. In the long run, this is what leads to the success of the company," said Chris.

"All the people who understood the significance of a brand are the ones who have created successful brands. Let me share with you a few brand stories that will help you relate to this concept better. To start off, let's talk about one of the biggest brands ever created—Nike," said Chris.

"Nike is a brand that has established an image of winning. Phil Knight, one of the co-founders of Nike, was a visionary. Nike is the world's most popular and biggest sportswear brand. It was a dream of

Phil Knight's to create better shoes, and today, Nike is worth more than thirty-four billion dollars. Phil Knight, a management graduate from Stanford University and also an athlete, knew very well that there was a big difference between being a management student and being an entrepreneur.

"He had once proposed in one of this business seminars in school, a paper titled, "Can Japanese Sports Shoes Do to German Sports Shoes What Japanese Cameras Did to German Cameras?" Japanese camera brands like Nikon and Canon had replaced all German cameras, and Knight wondered if the same could happen in the shoe industry. German brands Puma and Adidas were extremely popular in America during that time.

"After Phil graduated from school, he became obsessed with this idea of importing Japanese shoes to America and distributing them across the continent. Somewhere in his mind, he had a firm belief in his idea and didn't want it to die away like many other ideas do. He did not give up on his idea. Although he had no experience in any form of business, trading, or importing, he flew down to Japan in search of a good shoe brand. When he was in the city of Kobe, he came across a very popular Japanese shoe brand called Onitsuka Tiger. He had an acceptable technical understanding about shoes and realized that the shoes were of very high grade. He made up his mind to import this same brand to America.

"He fixed a meeting with the owner of Onitsuka Tiger. He was a highly confident young man and managed to convince the owner to give him the exclusive distribution for Onitsuka Tiger shoes for the region of the United States. His first consignment was for just twelve pairs of shoes, which he sold in one-on-one meetings. He soon realized that this mode of operation had scalability constraints and this would limit growth. That's when he remembered one person who understood shoes much more than he did, and Knight went to meet him. It was his former running coach at the University of Oregon—Bill Bowerman.

"Bill was a very popular American coach and had trained many big names. When Phil showed him these Tiger shoes, Bill fell in love with them, and he wanted to be a partner in the venture. Both of them incorporated the company Blue Ribbon Sports in 1964. Both of them invested $1,000 each in their company. With that money, they bought 300 pairs of Tiger shoes. Now, because of Bill's popularity, the shoes sold out within two months of arrival. Slowly, Tiger shoes started becoming popular in the United States, and their company expanded. They hired a new sales team. They opened their first retail showroom in 1965, and every time, the shoes would sell out before the consignment even reached the States.

"Bill was the technical person in the company who was doing all the research and innovation, whereas Phil looked into the business side of things. This combination was working out very well for both of them. With time, they realized that Onitsuka was unable to understand how big this brand would become in the United States and was focusing more on their local sales, leading to delay of consignments for them. Most of the time, the shoes were customized to Bill's innovations, and they worked great. One of the highest-selling designs of Tiger shoes, Cortez, was Bill's innovation. Soon, they realized that their growth was limited as a distributor, and they had a colossal dependency on Tiger shoes.

Billy was completely absorbed in the conversation. Chris wanted to take a quick break and picked up an apple. He quickly finished the apple, like he had a mission in hand, and got back into the Nike story.

"Once their contract with Tiger ended in 1972, they launched their own brand and named it Nike, after the goddess of victory. They started subcontracting all their production to different factories in Japan, and then they went on to be the biggest American sportswear brand in 1989. Part of Nike's success story involves endorsements by athletes such as Michael Jordan, Mia Hamm, Roger Federer, Tiger Woods, and many more. The Nike retail stores, the first of which opened in 1990, paid tribute to these athletes and offered their consumers a display of the full range of Nike products. By the early twenty-first century, Nike had retail outlets and distributors in more than 170 countries, and its logo—a curved check mark called the *swoosh*—was recognized throughout the world.

"Who in the world does not know Nike? This is the power of a brand. And a brand is created by people who are visionaries, people who understand the power of a brand. All their campaigns focused on just one message—winning. In all their campaigns, they showed a regular situation, then cut to a struggle, and then revealed how the survival instinct makes a winner.

"And today, they are the winner's brand," said Chris, summarizing this stunning story about Nike. "They created a promise to deliver. They created a beautiful story on winning. They created a perception of quality. They created a belief of being *en vogue*. They created a trust. And all these factors together created the exclusive identity of *Nike*. And that's called a brand," said Chris in a deep, powerful voice.

Billy had goosebumps. It had been an intensely inspiring story, and so well-narrated by Chris that Billy could feel himself being a part of the story. It was an exquisite example to explain to him the power of a brand. Billy's eyes were sparkling with excitement.

It was already 12:47 PM, and Chris decided to take a break. He picked up some juice and enjoyed the essence of the park while finishing their cigarettes. Then, Chris asked Billy, "Now do you understand the underlying potential of a brand?"

"Yes, sir. I got a very good insight. Until today, I underestimated the intensity of the term *brand*. But I've got it very clearly now. It's the brand that says it all," replied Billy.

"Yes. It's the brand that tells the success story," confirmed Chris. "Let me also quickly introduce you to an important term associated with a brand—*brand equity*. Some people also use this synonymously with *brand value*. Brand equity is a technical term that defines the value of the brand. It's mostly determined by the consumer perception about a brand. If a brand is highly popular then it has a positive brand value. And a positive brand value allows you to charge much higher for your product or services," added Chris.

"I guess Apple would have a great brand value?" asked Billy.

"Absolutely! Apple is a highly valuable brand, and that's why, for similar features and products, it's priced much higher than any of its competing brands," said Chris.

"But how do you arrive at brand value?" asked Billy.

"Every brand has a valuation as per the market capitalization. This is a combination of the tangible, measurable intangible, and intangible assets. You have to take out the tangible and the measureable intangible assets from the brand valuation, and that will give you the brand equity. This basically gives you a value premium of the brand, created over a period of time due to its consumer popularity," concluded Chris.

"So, what's the plan for lunch, Billy?" asked Chris.

"I haven't planned anything for the day. I was thinking of going with your plans," replied Billy.

"Ok, then. Let me take you for lunch to my friend's place. He owns a lovely little restaurant by the lake, and they're popular for their seafood. We can have lunch and continue with our conversation." suggested Chris.

"That sounds like a good plan. I would personally love to spend as much time as possible with you, as long as your time permits," said Billy.

They started moving out of the park. Smith called for the driver and picked up the basket. A black Lexus was waiting for them at the exit of the park. Smith helped Billy get into the car, and Smith put the wheelchair in the trunk of the car. He then hopped into the front seat, and they left for lunch.

The car stopped right in front of the entry of the restaurant. Smith helped Billy get into his wheelchair. Then, Smith and the driver left for lunch. Chris had asked Smith to book a private table by the water. The owner personally came over to greet Chris and showed them their table. The table was placed in a private corner with the best view, and their conversation would remain private.

Chris ordered a mimosa, and Billy ordered a beer. And, without wasting any time, Chris continued the conversation.

"I gave you a curtain raiser about what a brand means. It's very important to understand the power of the term *brand*. You have to ask yourself one question—whether you want to start a company or build a brand. Many novice entrepreneurs put in a lot of effort to build a new company, and they start their business in a haste, without focusing on the brand building process. Either they don't feel the importance, or they're ignorant about it. By not enforcing an extensive plan for the brand, they put their company into risk of failure. This might still be ok for a standalone, small-scale business. But if you're looking into scalability and creating a sizable brand, then you can't avoid this process," said Chris. He continued, "Tell me something, Billy. What's your idea about launching a new company?"

"Well, I've been thinking a lot about the kind of business I would like to start. I've not finalized the business idea, but I'm convinced about the fact that I would start my company only when I've an exclusive idea. I don't want it to be a run-of-the-mill idea. I would rather wait and invest more time in discovering a great business idea, instead of hurrying into the process of starting my company," replied Billy. "I also have to consider my financial constraints. So I need to think about a business model that may demand more time from me, but can be launched with a lesser investment. I'm trying to figure out a list of possible business ideas and slowly cross out what I feel is not so interesting or not doable. As soon as I zero in on my business idea, you'll be the first one to know about it. But, considering the limited available funds, it will mostly be a service-based brand that requires less investment."

"Good. I understand what you mean. It will not be an easy task for you to decide on a business with a very small investment," said Chris.

"I totally agree, Chris. But one good thing is that I know my practical situation, and I have to act accordingly. I don't mind working on an incremental model, where I start small and then slowly scale up," said Billy

"You know, kid, I've started liking the spark in you. Maybe it's because of the fact that you're very clear about what you want. That's why I feel that, one day, you can make it big," praised Chris.

"Thank you so much, Chris. You've been very kind to me, and words like these, coming from you, mean a lot to me. They motivate me and I have a strong feeling that I'm on the right path," Billy said courteously.

They chugged their drinks and got back to their conversation again. They didn't want to waste a single moment. It wasn't just Billy who was winning from this conversation. Chris was equally enjoying mentoring Billy.

***

Chapter 10

Lobster for Lunch

Your drive for creating a new and better world should be much bigger than your drive for becoming rich.

Chris and Billy were enjoying their drinks by the lake. They were recovering from a very extensive morning session. The owner of the restaurant dropped by their table for a courtesy visit. He was very glad to know that Chris was mentoring Billy, who had a great vision to do something meaningful in life.

They continued their conversation. "Now that you are still thinking about your business idea, just keep one very important factor in mind—make a difference. You're an intelligent entrepreneur, and you should think about making a difference to the existing social ecosystem," said Chris.

"Sorry, Chris, I don't understand. What does that mean?" asked Billy.

"Well, this sounds complicated, but it really isn't. Many entrepreneurs don't find it significant to understand the importance of being socially responsible, in making a difference to the world, in research and innovation. The drive to become rich is very high, and so is the risk of failing. You don't want your brand to take the same path," said Chris.

"There is a set pattern for all human beings, and we follow the patterns for our daily needs. You need to add a product or service into that pattern and make life easy for humans. That's what I call *changing the existing social ecosystem*. And that's when your brand will be respected and accepted globally easily. If you are able to crack this, then scalability, brand acceptance, loyalty, and, eventually, a successful brand are inevitable," said Chris.

"So, my golden words are, 'Your drive for creating a new and better world should be much bigger than your drive for becoming rich.'"

Chris repeated this very clearly, articulating each and every word, emphasizing every syllable as if to show how important this sentence would be for Billy in the future.

"I've never thought of this. Truth is that I was ignorant about this. This is an eye-opener for me. It makes so much sense, and it makes me question. Would anybody not think about this?" said Billy.

"Keeping it simple is always the toughest." Chris smiled.

"Which brands do you think have made a change to the social ecosystem?" asked Billy.

"Well, many brands have done this in a small or big format. But all those who fall in this league are profoundly successful brands. To name one of them, I would say Amazon. They changed the buying philosophy of the world. Nowadays, everything you want to buy is a click away, delivered at your doorstep. Before Amazon, we had to go to the supermarket or the retail showroom and pick it up ourselves. But now, we have the luxury of sitting at home and ordering the same thing online, and then utilizing our time in doing something more meaningful. This is what I mean by making a difference to the social ecosystem," said Chris.

Now Billy could very clearly relate to what Chris meant by "making a difference to the existing social ecosystem."

In the meantime, they'd finished with two rounds of drinks and appetizers, and it was 3:05 PM. The steward came to take the order for their main course. Chris ordered a special lobster dish for both of them. He wanted Billy to try his recommendation. Billy was so enthralled in the conversation that he was least bothered about his food, which was a pity, because the lobster was a restaurant special. He was so excited, he wished that this session would never end. Chris also ordered another drink and continued with their conversation.

"Uber would be another example. They revolutionized the mode of transportation, which is a basic human need. Nowadays, it's more convenient to take an Uber than to drive your own car. You may spend a long time finding parking. Even if you find a parking spot, you don't know how far that would be from your destination. Many times, it's disturbing to drive during peak hours. But Uber has resolved all these problems. You have a chauffeur-driven car on demand. Uber has taken it to the next level by creating an extraordinary user interface for better usability. This is a change to humanity," said Chris.

"Uber and Amazon are two examples of big changers, and there are many like them. They have created history and will be remembered forever. Like the big ones, there are many small-scale businesses who have contributed toward changing the current social ecosystem," added Chris.

After listening to Chris, Billy was completely pumped up and immediately dreamed about changing the world. He was highly motivated and enlightened. He felt that there was a whole new world that he'd been discovering every time he met Chris. He felt privileged that he'd gotten to meet Chris and had been exposed to a completely new horizon of knowledge.

Right on time, the steward brought their main dishes. The grilled lobsters looked exotic and were served with mashed potatoes and grilled veggies. The presentation was outstanding, and there was a sublime smell of grilled meat. Billy couldn't wait to dig in.

Chris continued the conversation while they ate. "I guess we had a huge lesson for one day. We should also take it easy so that you can go home, listen to our conversations, go through your notes, do more research, and build your own perception about everything you are learning. I never expect a yes-man student, as it gets very boring to just listen to *yes* all the time. You need a difference of opinion at times to rework your thoughts and come up with a brighter and better idea. So let's enjoy the lobster now and call it a day," said Chris.

Billy considered himself very fortunate to get so much time out of Chris's busy schedule. But he also knew that if Chris liked someone, then he really went all out.

Billy called Asha and told her that they would be done in twenty minutes. He sent the location of the restaurant. They were almost finished with their lunch when Asha came in and greeted Chris. Chris asked her to take a seat and ordered a chocolate mousse for her. Though she was working in his company, this was the first time Chris had met Asha.

In the next ten minutes, Chris's car was at the door. Chris said goodbye to both Billy and Asha and had started moving. Billy thanked him for such a splendid day and a great lunch.

As he was leaving, Chris told Billy, "By the way, Phil Knight himself wrote the book, *Shoe Dog*. If you like the Nike story, maybe you should get that book. Emilia will call you and let you know about our next meeting."

***

Chapter 11

A Beautiful Mind

Your thoughts are influenced by your mind. You do what your mind leads you to do. Devote all your energy in guiding your mind, and the rest will fall in place.

Billy always started his day with a well-designed workout and meditation session. Before the accident, Billy used to be a daily face in the gym, and that was the secret behind his outstanding physique. But now, he felt restricted, unable to complete his workout routines with just one leg. But that would not keep him away from working out and being fit. He researched many workout sessions for handicapped athletes and had slowly started following the same. So far, he had been enjoying the routines.

In the beginning, he was finding it difficult to practice any form of meditation for more than five minutes. His mind disagreed to stay focused. So he'd started with guided mediations and steadily progressed into long, deep meditation sessions. This helped him stay poised and allowed him to experience intellectual lucidity.

The latter part of his day was spent on research, reading, listening to Chris's audio tapes, and watching inspirational videos. He also started going out with his mother in the evenings, and would watch his mother guide the kids.

Their neighborhood was a mix of middle-class and struggling families. Many of the kids opted out from school and were leading aimless lives. It was very easy for kids like that to get influenced and take the sinful path. In fact, this had already happened with many of the kids in the past and had cost a few parents the lives of their kids. Understanding the pain of the families, Margaret had always been kind and devoted some of her time to these kids almost every day. Even the kids respected her for being so bold and selfless.

This made Billy understand how generous, authentic, and caring his mother was. He slowly started learning the art of giving. His mom used to say, "Real happiness is not in earning, but in giving. Whatever little you have, or whatever little you know, keep sharing. Just think how beautiful this world will be when everybody starts giving and sharing."

Before the accident, Billy used to think that his parents were ignorant about real life and happiness. But now that he was part of the small acts of giving, and staying close to his family, he'd started understanding his mistakes and that the real happiness of life was in making others happy.

Billy started catching up with his friends whenever he was free from his family, books, and research. He wanted to take Sean to We Care. Sean had never been to any such place before, but agreed to go because Billy insisted. Billy was convinced that Sean would surely have something positive to take home from there.

One evening, Sean picked up Billy from his home, and they both went to We Care. All the people already knew Billy very well, as he was a regular. Sean was a little hesitant in the beginning and not sure how he should react. He stayed close to Billy and looked around the place. They got some chocolates and cookies for the kids, who were very happy to see Billy back. The kids thanked them. Billy started talking to the kids, and Sean also started mingling with them.

One of the kids came over to Sean and sat on his lap and asked him to explain the solar system. Sean smiled and started explaining it to her. She had endless questions, but Sean was very patient and answered them all. After talking to him for almost twenty minutes, she was delighted that she now knew all about the galaxy. She went running to her friends and started sharing what she'd just learned.

Sean realized that all the kids were so used to caring and sharing that it was not just the food, they shared everything, even knowledge. He could see that they were extremely happy and content. Most of them had their smiles on. They didn't have their own families, but had learnt how to be part of a bigger family. They'd mastered the art of finding reasons to be happy rather than being sad.

Sean and Billy stayed there until dinner. On their way back, Sean thanked Billy. "Thank you, bro, for bringing me to We Care. I never expected to be so emotionally touched by these kids. They are brilliant. And look at me. I have everything in life, and yet I'm searching for happiness every moment of my life. I don't understand."

"That's the irony of life, my brother. Some have everything, but don't see it. Some have nothing, but find happiness everywhere. It's all in our minds, whether we want to be happy or not. We always have two choices—keep complaining about what we don't have, or else find our happiness from whatever little we do have. Choice is always ours," said Billy.

"So, you mean to say that whenever I am sad or dejected, it's not because of the situation around me, but because of the way I'm thinking?" asked Sean.

"Yes, it is. Any human gets affected by an adverse situation around them, but that's temporary. A strong and balanced mind comes out of that momentary gloom much quicker. Whatever has happened has already happened, and now it's completely on us whether we want to be sorry about the past or get over it and fight back positively," said Billy.

"I'm also very new to this. I never had an understanding about the philosophical truth of life. But now, I'm learning and getting better every day. Whatever I'm speaking is from the very little knowledge that I've gathered over the past few months. I've started realizing the importance of a positive mind, and I'm glad that you're feeling positive as well." Billy smiled.

Sean said nothing. He was trying to understand his new experience. He felt enlightened. He felt a sense of inner joy. He was filled with gratitude for Billy for helping him experience this. They reached Billy's house and Sean asked, "Is it ok if we get a beer at your place?"

"Yes, for sure. Please come over," said Billy.

The Grahams were having dinner when they came in. Billy asked them to continue with their plans and told them that he would have dinner in a while. He picked up two pints of beer from the refrigerator and went out to the lawn.

"Sorry I gate-crashed for a beer," said Sean.

"That's perfectly fine. Even I'm enjoying my beer, thanks to you," said Billy.

"What you said was so powerful. I just wanted to wait for some time, absorb it, and then go home," said Sean.

"Bro, I don't want to sound like a saint, but I have to tell you that some of the things you're doing aren't right. I was in the same boat a few months ago. I never realized this then. But now, I understand what we were doing then wasn't right. So I'm taking the liberty of advising you to come out of all of this. There's nothing we can achieve from it. No matter how much money you earn, there will always be an emptiness in your mind. Your mind will always be wandering and looking for happiness and peace. And I'm sure you don't want that. Maybe you can start looking at life with a new perspective," advised Billy.

"I got the point about the mind, and I kind of agree with you. But how to control this mind?" asked Sean.

"The mind is like a game. The more you train, the better you get. You need to start meditating. Your mind is always looking for a clear medium to help you become a better person. But, most of the time, it's cluttered. In that case, the mind starts working against you. It's your mind, and you need to help your mind to help you. You can achieve this only by decluttering and stabilizing your mind," said Billy.

"In the beginning, you will find it difficult, and your mind will wander a lot. But you have to be patient. You will soon realize that you're progressing in stabilizing your mind. It's all about persistence, and that's what many of us lack. We start a new activity with a lot of energy and expect immediate results. But that's not how it happens. Any new habit takes time, and many of us give up before it becomes a regular habit. So, believe in yourself, and keep working toward guiding your mind," said Billy.

Sean was highly motivated by Billy's words. Billy had been in a similar state of mind a few months back, and he had trained his mind so well within this short period of time. This thought gave Sean the inspiration that if he were disciplined and honest, he could also train his mind the same way. With a fulfilled and positive mindset, Sean left for the night, thanking Billy for everything.

***

Chapter 12

The Unexplored Ocean

Every successful brand has a beautiful story. Every beautiful story has a loyal following.

Friday evening at 8:00 PM, Billy met Chris at the port. He'd tried hard to figure out what Chris had planned there.

"Hey, Chris. So good to see you. Hope you had a nice week," greeted Billy.

"Hey, Billy. How have you been? I had a very hectic week, so I decided to take it easy this evening," replied Chris.

"Oh! I hope I'm not bothering you."

"No, absolutely not. This is more of a break for me. No stress at all," assured Chris.

"Where are we going?" asked a curious Billy.

"Well, I thought you'd let me give you a small surprise," said Chris, grinning.

Chris started walking into the port, and Billy followed him. They came to a place where all the private yachts were parked. Billy thought, *Is this for real? Are we that going to spend the evening on a yacht?* He knew this was happening when he spotted Smith, welcoming them to one of the lovely looking, medium-sized yachts. He had made arrangements to allow wheelchair access into the yacht. They entered, and Smith greeted Billy with a great smile and asked, "How have you been doing, sir? Hope you had a great week."

"Hey, Smith. I've been super good, and thanks for your amazing hospitality all the time. I really appreciate it," said Billy.

The yacht was a chic mix of pure-white body and black, tinted glass. It could house thirty to thirty-five people and was spread across two floors. As soon as you entered the yacht from the rear end, there was a small jacuzzi opening onto a wooden deck, where around twenty sofas were arranged. The sofas were aqua blue. The space was covered with black, tinted glass on three sides, with the back left completely open. Toward the front, at the end of the deck, was a retro-looking Irish wooden bar, crafted beautifully to go with the contemporary design of the yacht. Smith had made arrangements for a lounge setup for them on the lower deck. And to create the right mood, he also played some Simon and Garfunkel classics. The upper deck was partially open from the top and completely open from all the sides. It had less seating, but anyone standing there could immerse themselves in the water and breeze.

Both of them seated themselves on the lower deck. Chris asked Smith for some water and his regular drink, Scotch on the rocks with a lemon wedge. Billy wanted to take it easy and asked for a virgin mojito to start with. Chris asked the captain to take the yacht into deep water.

"Welcome to my second home, Billy," said Chris.

"So, I'm guessing this is your own private yacht? Pardon my ignorance. These kind of luxuries are difficult for me to even imagine," said Billy innocently.

"Yes, it's my own yacht. But I only use it occasionally. In the beginning, you feel great about it, but very soon, you realize that it was one of your passing desires. I wanted to meet you in a new place, and hence, opted for the yacht. Also, I thought it would be an exciting experience for you." Chris smiled.

"Anyway, you tell me how your week was. And what new have you tried this week?" continued Chris.

"It was a good week. I listened to last week's voice notes over and over again. I went through my written notes. I bought the book *Shoe Dog* and started reading it," replied Chris.

"Besides that, personally, I started exercising and meditating every day, and that's helping me stay positive and gives me a better perspective in understanding the real person within. I also took my friend Sean to We Care this week, and we had long conversations about being optimistic and learning to control our minds. Sean has been involved in a few shady activities, and I'm trying to help him get away from them," said Chris.

"I also spent a lot of time with my family and few evenings with my mom in the neighborhood. My mom actually gives sermons to young guys in the evenings to show them the right path in life. Ironically, I'd never spoken to her in that capacity any time before my accident," Billy said, smiling.

"Looks like you had a busy week. But I'm impressed to hear about your weekly activities every time. Last week, you learned the art of forgiving, and this week, you started sharing your experience and knowledge with your friends. Great going, Billy. I'm already proud of you," praised Chris.

"Have you ever thought about why I'm taking out so much time for you, even though I have a tight schedule at work?" asked Chris gently, smiling with crinkled eyes.

"I read about you, Chris, and now I'm getting to know you personally. You're very grounded and kindhearted, especially when it comes to helping people. You feel that you want to give back in some way, big or small," replied Billy.

"Well, you're partly right. Here's another fact you won't find about me on the 'net. When I started my business, I desperately wanted some mentoring, but I was left to burn my hands and learn. It's a great way of learning, but I could have done much better during my starting phase, or avoided many mistakes, if somebody—the right person—would have mentored me. Ever since then, I promised myself that whenever I could, I'd try to help people like me. I believe that whatever little we know, we must share. If we start sharing, most of our problems can be prevented, instead of being cured later," said Chris in an honest tone. His voice revealed that he hoped this wish would come true. This reminded Billy of his mother, who always said the same thing.

Chris got up from his comfortable sofa and started walking towards the bar. He asked for his drink to be refilled. There was a live BBQ next to the bar, and a chef was grilling some prawns and chicken skewers. The yacht had travelled for some distance, and was now anchored in the middle of nowhere. All you could see was water on all four sides, with some shimmering lights in the distance. The lights from the yacht lit the water around it. It could have been an ideal romantic moment with a partner, but here we had two gentlemen talking about management and the good life. Chris stood by the railing, looking at the mighty lake Michigan, and Billy sat on a chair next to him, taking in the beauty of the calm, deep water.

"In our last meeting, we spoke about what a brand is, as well as making a difference to the social ecosystem. Let's take it from there, all right? Do you have any questions about our last conversation?" asked Chris politely, allowing Billy to understand the importance of what was coming his way.

"Erm, no, we're good to go ahead. I'll ask you whenever I have any questions," replied Billy.

"Today we're going to talk about something very crucial—the important factors to be considered before launching any brand or business. The success of a brand depends on how comprehensive your brand launch plan is. If you follow these factors, or pointers, then I guess you won't miss out on anything essentially required for launching a brand," said Chris.

Billy was very thrilled to hear the topic of the day. As usual, he started recording voice notes and got his note pad and pen ready.

Chris continued the conversation. He was now framing how he wanted to explain the entire subject to Billy in an easy-to-understand manner.

"These factors are purely based on my experience with the hundreds of brands that I've worked with during my career. This may not tally with some of the books in the market or internet content, as there's no template or any thumb rule. So let's dive right in."

Billy was concentrating so hard that his eyebrows were literally kissing each other. Chris continued in a calm-yet-intense manner.

"According to me, the most important points that you need to take care of before launching a brand are brand purpose, brand definition, set up and infrastructure planning, knowing and reaching your targeted group, developing sales and marketing strategies, business planning, culture and brand constitution. Let me introduce you to all these eight points briefly, and then we can talk about each point in detail. For today, I guess we can finish the overview of all these factors, and then we would need to discuss each factor in detail starting from our next session," explained Chris.

"Sure," said Billy. "As you wish."

Chris continued, "Last time we spoke about a brand making a difference to the social ecosystem. The first—and the most important—point for you to understand is the *purpose* of a brand. This is the big *why* behind the brand. Things have changed in today's business world. When I started my agency, we never had such stiff competition, and hence, the probability of success was much higher. Now, the market is very cluttered, and everybody is screaming at the top of their voices. And all have one message—to sell. So it becomes very important for you to have your Unique Selling Proposition (USP), or differentiators, as we call them. But a brand needs much more than just a USP to stand out in a crowded world. And what they need is a *purpose*, which is the *brand story*. This, Billy, is what helps a brand win the loyalty of its customers."

Chris asked for his drink to be refilled. He also asked for a glass of gin and tonic for Billy. They went to the BBQ area and served themselves some grilled prawns. The yacht was at a standstill, gently drifting along the water. At that moment, Billy felt that he was the most fortunate man in the world. He wished that, someday, he could do this for someone else, just the way Chris had done for him. They picked up their drinks, moved back to the lounge on the deck, and sat down comfortably. Smith helped Billy with his drink and seated him comfortably. Chris was maintaining his momentum, and, without wasting any more time, he continued.

"Now that you know the purpose of the brand, let's move to the second point—the product. The brand definition is a whopping topic in itself and involves numerous activities like naming the product, the logo, brand vision, brand mission, positioning of the product, designing of the logo, brand identity, and finally, development of the product. Your brand can be a product or a service, but before launching the brand, it's very important to understand the brand definition. The brand definition has to be very well-researched, and only then should it be defined," said Chris.

"I'm sure you'll have lots of questions, and we can discuss them when we further delve into each point. An introduction to these pointers will give you a better understanding of the topics, and you'll be able to correlate when we are discussing each one of them in detail. Now, moving on to the next point, setup and infrastructure planning. In this section, you would need to define your setup cost, infrastructure needs, processes, operation flow charts, and your human resources. This has to fall in line with your capital. If you're planning to start a business with a low capital, then it's very important to spend a lot of time in this section to identify the optimal use of your capital. A business, once started, should never get stuck halfway before it's launched or during the initial days of operation. That's a pure waste of money. So you have to ensure that, before you start any business, you have enough capital to start sailing with a minimum operational cost of six months," added Chris

They were interrupted by Smith, who came in to inform Chris that he had to attend to an urgent call. It was 11:00 PM, and Billy hadn't even realized that three hours had gone by. He stood up with the help of his crutches and took a small, slow stroll toward the railings. He stood there and embraced the artistry of the tranquil waters. He asked Smith for another drink. He wondered about how, earlier, when he wasn't handicapped and had had the physical ability to do whatever he wanted, he'd been mentally trapped.

Now, even though he was physically challenged, his mind had become so optimistic that his physical state did not define what he could or could not do. He thought about many people in this world who felt that they were physically fit and could do whatever they wanted, but never realized that they were actually mentally stymied. Their mind was deceiving them and making them live in a mysterious, virtual world.

Everything had seemed right to Billy earlier, so much so that he'd been ready to take shortcuts in his life just to become rich. There'd been no conscience holding him back from doing evil acts. He was completely blinded by his own reflections and convictions. He wished that he could show the reality to people like him who were still living in darkness.

As he was lost in his thoughts and was tussling between his past and present, Chris came over and interrupted. "Enjoying the peace?"

Billy was taken by surprise and broke out of his reverie, but soon smiled and replied, "Yes, Chris. This is so heavenly. I was just thinking. We're so petty at times. We have everything we need right in front of us, but we stay blindfolded and keep looking for them in other things. We are bizarre and utterly stupid most of the times."

Chris smiled as if he were convinced with this statement. He asked Smith for a repeat. He also asked Billy to help himself to whatever he wanted to eat. He then asked Billy, "Are you glad we met at this yacht"?

"Absolutely, Chris! I dreamt many times to be on a private yacht, talking to my friends and enjoying the immaculate beauty of the still water. And here I am, on a private yacht with the person I respect and admire the most, gearing up for a bright future. So I guess this is an ideal moment for me," replied Billy.

"Also, I never ever considered myself to be so blessed, until now. I'm experiencing amazing luxuries while being mentored. I guess my stars are well-aligned," laughed Billy.

"It's all in our minds. I'm glad you've started feeling this way." Chris smiled.

It was almost 11:30 PM, and they decided to continue the rest of the conversation. Chris said, "Let's move to the fourth point, know and reach your target group. The target group defines the *for whom* for a brand. You have to understand the positioning of a brand and know your TG. This is the key to being focused, creating the right content and the right communication. Not every brand in the world is made for everybody in the world. Every brand has its own targeted crowd. The business model has to be in sync with the positioning.

Many brands don't define the TG clearly and get tempted to cater to everyone, which might lead to brand failure. It's actually a very simple, known fact—no brand in the world has ever been able to cater to all. So why would you think about doing it? Once you're aware of your TG, the next step is to determine how to make your product or service reach that TG. The path of making your product reach your client is called the *distribution channel*. Your channels can be direct or indirect, depending on your business model."

Billy had a few questions, but he saved them for the detailed sessions. He kept recording and taking notes. He treasured these notes.

"Moving to the fifth point, a practical business plan needs to be detailed out before the launch of the brand. A small part of it can be considered after the launch. A business plan would talk more about the fund flow of the company. The growth of the brand is dependent on the business plan. The right amount of funds has to come into the company at the right time, else your activities would be put on hold. A comprehensive business plan allows you to sail your business smoothly toward success. Whether you are starting a small business or expanding an existing one, your business plan would be the road map to success. It also helps you keep a check on your planned timelines versus reality," explained Chris.

They ordered for another round of drinks. Chris always loved to take small breaks to keep it interesting. They also ordered for some more appetizers and salads, as they had missed dinner that day. Chris would bring in lots of examples of his personal experience as an entrepreneur. These examples motivated Billy because he realized the real connect and how Chris fought against all odds to come out a winner in every situation.

"Next, we'll talk about sales and marketing strategies, which are the most critical factors for a successful brand. The marketing strategies start getting formalized post business planning where you have allocated a certain budget for marketing activities for the whole year. Many times, it's a cyclic process where the business plan changes due to the budgeting of the marketing activity. Marketing strategies would include a very big scope of work—creating all content, define the tone of communication for the brand, strategies, channels of communication and timelines. It also defines the brand goals and the process of achieving those goals. The sales strategies are thoroughly revenue driven and the strategies to reach the company targets. Both the strategies are highly dependent on each other—sales needs marketing support to reach their target, and marketing needs sales to drive the brand activities more," explained Chris.

"Now I am coming to two of my favorites, culture and brand constitution. The culture defines the personality of the brand. It defines the organizational environment. An employee in any company spends more time at work than at home. A good culture should be an inevitable part of the brand because it's the people who build the brand, and it's extremely important for them to love their workplace. They're the most loyal brand advocates in the real sense. Companies make it a mission to satisfy their customers, but many don't know how to achieve it. Most importantly, as a brand, you should always work toward satisfying your people, and if they're satisfied and happy, you don't have to worry about your customers. They'll be taken care of by the people. Isn't that simple? But still, many brands don't get this right. Now, why does the culture definition become very important before the launch of the brand? That's because the brand culture always flows from top to bottom. If you practice the culture from the beginning, then it starts flowing into the team by itself. It's very difficult to create a new culture with an old team in the same brand. It's the brand culture that ties each and every personnel in the company," said Chris.

"The last one is a self-made one. I did this for my brand, and then I made many other brands do it, and to my knowledge, each and every one of them have benefited from this. Would you like to take a guess on what I mean by *brand constitution*?" asked Chris.

"I'm not sure, but I guess it's the company document," replied Billy.

"I'm not referring to a company official document, which is a mandate while forming the company. You can call this a bible for the brand. This document defines the top-level policies of the brand during the inception of the brand. Many times, the drive for increasing profits make a brand drift away from its core values. With the brand-constitution document in place, the management already has a defined path, especially in moments of conflict. Neither the employees nor the founders can change the brand-constitution document. It can be modified only when all the active founders unanimously agree to the changes. This is what I've been practicing, and many times, even without wanting to do things in a particular way, I had to do it because of this document, which benefited me in a big way in the long run. This document should be an essential for every company, irrespective of being a single founder or a multiple founder company," explained Chris.

"Umm! That was quite a lot of talking. What do you say, Billy?" asked Chris.

"Well, it must be really tiring for you. Now, it's 12:45 AM, which means you've been speaking for more than four hours. But for me, this moment passed in the blink of an eye and I can't explain how much I learned today. Every single day spent with you is like an ocean of knowledge. Thank you so much, Chris," said Billy with lot of respect.

"Hey, Smith, I need a strong one now," said Chris, smiling, and he asked for a refill of his drink as if a mission was accomplished for the day.

Smith got a refill of both the drinks for Chris and Billy. He also got some jamóns and cheese to go with them. Both Chris and Billy moved to a bar table on the deck. They both lit their cigarettes and were captivated by the gentle breeze.

Billy broke the silence. "Someone rightly said, 'Smell the sea, feel the breeze, listen to the water, be at ease.' Sir, I'd like to mention once more that today was wonderful. I am thankful to you and I know that I can never repay you for what you are doing for me."

Chris laughed and said, "You're always like this, so formal, or you are trying to impress me?"

Billy smiled and let the silence speak for itself.

It was 1:00 AM, Chris asked the captain to take the yacht back to the port. They reached the port in twenty minutes. Billy had booked his regular cab that was waiting for him by the port. Billy got into the cab and Chris in his car. Billy was so overwhelmed. He had no words to define this lovely evening.

***

Chapter 13

Stay Close to Nature

Nature is filled with unconditional love for humanity. Stay close to nature.

The same Sunday, the Grahams decided to go out for a picnic. It had been a while since they'd all gone out together. John was, as usual, busy with his work. Margaret joined her school again after it reopened. Asha had been very busy with her internship, and Billy had also been busy with his mentoring sessions and research work. They had lot of catching up to do, and like every time, Asha took the initiative of deciding the venue and itinerary for the day.

They finished breakfast and enjoyed their coffee in their lawn. Margaret checked with Asha if she needed to prepare anything for the picnic. Asha said, "Mom, we don't need to carry anything at all. You will know when we get there." The family was a little surprised about this picnic they were headed to, where they weren't carrying anything to eat or drink.

They drove down deep into the suburbs and finally into the fields. As they drove through, they could see many cars parked. They parked and got out of their car. There were many trees separating the parking from the destination where a lot of people were assembled. They slowly walked past the trees, with Asha controlling Billy's wheelchair, and soon saw that there was a big, beautiful lake. The water was clean and clear, so clear you could see your own reflection. On their left, they saw many temporary white canvas pergolas. There was a huge BBQ where they were grilling whole fish and different kinds of meat. There was a separate counter for craft beer and house wine, and there were many more counters for food and games.

It was a special Sunday, as the farmers were celebrating their first crop. Around the lake, the grass was lush green, and there were many beautiful patches of trees and shrubs. Next to the pergolas, there was a wooden ramp running into the lake where some people were feeding fish. It was such a lovely setup that the Grahams were pleasantly surprised and very happy to be there.

Asha and Margaret got some white wine, and the men picked up some beer. They also got some grilled fish and chicken and went near the lake. They were carrying a big table mat that they placed on the grass with the food and the drinks on it. Billy laid himself down on the soft lush green carpet of grass and gazed at the clear blue sky. The feeling was so serene that he wished time would stop and this moment would freeze forever. The splendor of nature captivated his soul, and he was in a happy, tranquil state of mind.

The whole family was silent for a while, gazing at the sky, taking in beauty of the clear water, and watching the trees swoosh with their beautiful colored flowers.

"I feel good. Everything looks so nice. The birds, the water, the grass, the clear blue sky, the trees, the fresh breeze," expressed Billy with a lot of joy.

"You know; nature is the second best thing I always liked after my family. When I was young and unmarried, in fact since my childhood, I used to run into the fields, forests, lakes, and spend hours and hours sitting there," John said.

"Grandpa and Grandma never yelled at you because you would disappear for hours?" asked Asha.

"No, not at all. They themselves were profound lovers of nature and used to spend a lot of time in forests and parks. Your Grandpa use to say, 'Son, always be with nature. It reminds us where we belong. It hugs us with love whenever we are feeling low. It speaks to us whenever we want to be in peace. It heals and helps us start over again.' And that's how I fell in love with nature," John replied.

Margaret said, "Nature never fails you. It will always ensure that it brings peace and tranquility to you. But we human beings have stopped respecting nature. In our desperate drive for modernization, we've started abusing nature. There's no point of this mad rush when there is no peace, no happiness, no emotions."

"We used to have smaller goals in life like, running in the fields with friends, roasting a meal in the forest, going out with family, playing with friends, and it was so easy for us to achieve these smaller goals. And as a result, we were happy all the time. It never mattered how much money we had. But now, everybody has such high goals, and most of the time, they never achieve them. And even if they achieve it, they set even higher goals to ensure that finally they don't achieve them. Don't you think that's ironic? We all are running this rat race trying to find happiness, but we ourselves don't want to be happy," added John.

Asha was moved by what John had said, but wanted to have clarity on a few things. She said, "Maybe things are not as they seem to you. Our generation has grown up in a different environment, where life is competitive. We also love nature, but our priority is definitely not nature. We are more focused on being successful, and there are many people who are successful and happy. What do you have to say about that?"

John replied, "I'm not saying that your generation is wrong. Your generation was shown this path by our generation. The root cause is us. We couldn't maintain the balance and let your generation inherit the strong bond between humans and nature. Or maybe things changed so much that we never realized that our focus shifted toward achieving luxuries. Many like me failed to achieve that in a big way as we always had our feet on two boats. But all we can do now is share our experiences with the younger generation, how things were in the past and how happiness was so easily achievable. And that's what I'm doing today."

"Dad, you never failed us. You always did your best. Even though many times we felt that other people lived more luxuriously than us, but we understand reality. You've been the best dad, always lending a patient ear and your time, standing next to us whenever we needed you. You never hesitated to forgive us whenever we did something wrong. You hugged us even tighter to ensure that we felt safe. So please don't feel bad about anything. Both of us believe that we have the best parents. And if at any moment we've said we weren't happy, that was our foolishness and a desperate attempt to cover our own failures," said Billy.

Margaret, as always, was almost in tears, but managed to hold them back. She didn't want her family making fun of her again. But she was glad to see so much love.

"Thank you, my son, for reassuring us that we did well if not great. Margaret and I, we always loved you both. It never mattered to us how you were and what you did. Many times, we were tough on both of you because we wanted to show you the right path. Most importantly, both of us feel very proud and lucky to have children like you," said John.

Everyone was emotional and happy at the same time that they could speak their heart. This was the magic of nature, which opens up all your emotions. John tried to change the topic back to nature and said, "Well, coming back to the topic, I would like to advise you both to take out some time for nature, no matter what you are doing at any point of your life. We are as busy as we think we are. We can always take out time for things we love, otherwise there is no meaning to this beautiful life. You need to decide whether you want to live like robots or cherish the heavenly beauty of Mother Nature.

"In today's world, there has been excessive abuse towards nature. Many times, we become so selfish that we just care about our happiness and leave the evils to nature. If we continue doing this, there'll be a day when things are going to come back to us the same way. So I'll be extremely glad if you guys work toward restoring our beautiful planet and do your bit, whenever you have time," continued John.

"I had many downs in my life, and whenever I didn't know what to do, I would immerse myself and surround myself by nature and spend endless hours. All I can remember is that, every time, I would go back with a peaceful mind. The bond you share with nature is serene and the more time you spend, the more you are at peace," concluded John.

The grilled fish was out of this world. Asha and John went to refill their drinks and get some more fish. The Grahams sat by the lake and spoke about things happening in their individual lives. Billy had a lot of interesting things to share with them about Chris and his lessons. The family was immensely touched by Chris for the way he had been inspiring and mentoring Billy. For some time, Billy and John slept on the grass while Asha and Margaret went for a walk by the lake.

They spent the whole afternoon by the lake. They had some hot dogs for lunch from one of the counters. It was a great day for the family specially because they could talk and share so many things. They all loved nature and believed that they would always keep the connection strong.

***

Chapter 14

The Unforgettable Trip

Planning leads to expectations. Make an unplanned trip and be surprised to have your best moments.

Monday morning, 11:00 AM, Emelia called Billy. "Hey, Billy, how have you been? Are your enjoying your sessions with Chris?"

"Hey, Emelia, I'm doing good. Thank you so much. Yes, the sessions are very interesting, and I'm having a great time with Chris. I guess I'm the lucky one to be mentored by Chris. He's a great guy," replied Billy.

"Well, guess what. I have a great surprise for you," said Emelia.

"Really? I'm excited and can't wait to hear it. Last time, your surprise, it was mind blowing. So what's happening this time?" asked Billy.

"Can't say much. It's a surprise. Please check with your family if you can travel from Friday until Monday," said Emilia.

"Are you serious, Emilia?" Billy felt a chill in his body.

"Yes, I'm always serious, and I tell you what I'm asked to," explained Emilia.

"Let me call you back this evening or tomorrow morning. I need to discuss this with my family. I'd love to go wherever Chris wants me to. I haven't stepped out of town after my accident, so it would be better to check and get back to you," said Billy.

"I can understand. However, we have taken care of your safety, and Smith would be traveling with you in the same flight. If you agree to go, then Smith will meet you with your ticket at the airport," concluded Emilia.

"I have one more question. How much should I pay for the tickets and travel? I need to check this with my dad as well," asked Billy.

"Oh! Don't worry about that. Chris wouldn't take any money from you. He's doing this at his own will," explained Emilia.

"That's so nice of him, but I don't feel good about it. He's already helping me so much, and on top of that, he's spending all this money. Maybe someday I'll be capable enough to give back the way he'd like," said Billy.

"You do well in your life, and that would be the best you could give back to Chris," said Emilia with a smile and hung up the call.

Billy kept wondering about the trip all the time and was very excited. He would have said yes to Emilia at that moment itself, but now he wasn't completely confident because of his physical disability. Though he had managed to be completely independent at home, the thought of being outside home for three days made him worry. Billy spoke to his parents over dinner the same day and told them about Emilia's phone call. Margaret looked a little hesitant, but John and Asha were very excited.

John said, "That's great news. You should surely go and join Chris. He's a responsible man, and I'm sure he would have thought through this."

Asha smiled. "Yeah, me too. I'm so jealous of you, Billy. My boss, who just met me once, is taking you all around. You're so lucky."

"That's it? That was quick. I've been worried and thinking about this the whole day. And here, you guys just decided everything within seconds. Well, I guess I should go then." Billy grinned.

He texted Emilia immediately. "I'm in."

"But where are you going?" asked Asha.

"No idea. Chris wanted it to be a surprise," Billy replied.

Asha laughed. "I'm sure it's going to be some amazing place. That's why he's keeping it a surprise. Oh! I'm more jealous now. Please ask Chris if I can join next time."

Friday morning, 7:00 AM, Billy met Smith outside O'Hare International airport. Their flight was at 8:45 AM.

"Hello, sir, how have you been?" asked Smith.

"Hey, Smith, I'd prefer you calling me Billy. 'Sir' is too heavy for me. I'm doing great. Hope you're good too," Billy replied.

"Sure, Billy," said Smith, smiling warmly.

"So, now may I finally know where are we going?" Billy asked.

"Absolutely! We're flying to Miami. But where in Miami, you'll know soon. To be honest, even I don't know that," Smith replied.

"Oh wow! Really? The surprise couldn't have been better," said Billy excitedly with a smile.

"Billy, you're with Mr. Chris. He's a guy with a big heart, and if he likes someone, he's very genuine with that person, and I guess you're lucky to be on that list."

The flight landed in Miami at 1:15 PM. They came out of the airport, and there was a man holding a placard for Billy. Normally, you'd expect a guy dressed as a driver, a black suit with a cap maybe. But this guy was different. He was huge, probably six three dressed in torn jeans, a black T-shirt topped with a leather jacket, high black boots, and a black baseball cap, dressed like a dude.

Billy went to the guy and identified himself.

"Hello, my name is Ron, and I'm here to pick you up," said Ron with a very firm handshake to both Billy and Smith. Smith was also traveling to Miami for the first time. Ron had a thick, husky voice that went very well with his physique. Both Billy and Smith looked at each other, smiled, and followed Ron.

To Billy's surprise, there was a sparkling black Hummer waiting for them. Ron opened the trunk and helped them put the luggage and Billy's wheelchair and crutches in the trunk. Billy sat in the front seat, with Ron driving the beast. Billy couldn't wait to see where they were going. This trip was turning out to be a fairy tale for him. Every moment had a new surprise in store for him, and it was beyond real. A Hummer is every young boy's fantasy, especially the tough ones, and Billy surely was one of them. Ron started driving and Billy was super excited to be in Miami. As they drove through the city, Billy could see the fun side of the city, especially when they drove past South Beach Road. People were enjoying themselves, and all the restaurants were packed for lunch. You could see people mostly in their beach wear, dressed up casually and enjoying the lovely weather.

They kept driving for forty-five minutes until they entered a smaller road. The road was heading toward the beach, and they finally reached a black gate. Ron opened the gate with the remote control, and as the gate opened, Billy could see a big lawn with a driveway, and at the end of the lawn was a highly contemporary, two-storied white glass villa. Ron stopped the vehicle right in front of the villa and helped Billy get down and got him seated in his wheelchair.

"Welcome to Mr. Adams's villa in Miami. My name is Sam, and I'm the caretaker of this villa," said Sam, who came to receive them at the porch.

Oh wow, this looks like a great place, Billy thought and couldn't wait to explore the villa.

The main door, which was around fifteen feet in height, opened into a long, double-height, pure-white living space. As Billy walked, he could see that it was decked with pure white sofas and glass on both the sides of the living room. On the right, the double-height glass opened to a back porch with a huge dining table, opening into the pool. On the left, the half-glass partition separated the guest rooms at the rear end with a glass staircase going up between the rooms and the half-glass partitions. At the end of the living room was one more long dining table close to a white, open island kitchen. To the right of the dining and kitchen spaces was the same porch running all the way till the end. The kitchen connected internally to a small kitchen and BBQ on the outside section. The plain frameless glass that formed the right wall made the living, dining, and the kitchen part of the open pool. Billy went out of the living room to the pool and saw the magnificent view facing the ocean. The view was stunning, and Billy for a moment couldn't believe that he was inside such a colossal villa, which was beyond his fantasies. On both sides of the pool, there were lush green lawns, almost touching the water. At the center of the lawn, there was a wooden pathway going up the deck to the water, where a yacht was parked.

Sam showed Billy his room, which was just behind the staircase on the left side of the living room. The room was spacious and the wooden flooring added a feeling of warmth. The bedroom was minimalistic in design, with white being the dominant color. The wall behind the bed had a raw cement finish, and the curtains were matte black, backed by light-gray sheer fabric. The collapsible glass partition between the room and balcony, opening to the green lawn gave the room a bigger feel. The toilet was also equally spacious and had two shower areas—one indoor and one open to the sky. It also had a small jacuzzi perfect for two under the sky.

"Sir, hope you liked your room," asked Sam.

"Absolutely! Thank you so much for showing me around and getting me here," replied Billy.

Ron came inside the house and met Billy in the living room. "Mr. Adams is busy the whole day with meetings and will be back by 7:00 PM. He asked me to check if you are comfortable here. He also asked you to enjoy lunch in-house and get some rest since you traveled a lot today. Please feel free to use the bar. Smith will help you with that."

Ron went out of the villa, got into the car, and left. Sam introduced Billy to Chef Tom, who had been working in this villa for the last three years. Billy preferred eating at the breakfast counter and Tom was cooking some salads and chicken steaks. Billy was chatting with Tom while he was cooking. He learned that Chris had bought this villa almost four years ago. He mostly works two days out of his Miami office every week. Tom also told him that lot of celebrities and successful businessmen came to this villa for social get-togethers. The lunch was heavenly. Billy thanked Tom for it.

It was almost 4:00 PM, and Billy decided to crash for some time and get fresh before Chris's arrival.

Billy's alarm rang at 6:00 PM sharp. The room was completely dark, and when he woke up, he was in an uncertain state of mind, and it took him few seconds to realize where he was and what the time was. Slowly, he came out of his trance confused state and realized that he was at this lovely villa in Miami that belonged to Chris and that he had a meeting with him in the evening. It had been an insanely thrilling day for him, and now he was excited that he was going to meet Chris very soon.

Billy quickly got fresh and ready for the evening. He came out of his room and asked Tom for a strong cup of coffee and sat by the pool. Tom got it in a jiffy, and Billy was all by himself, experiencing the hypnotic moment in one of the best places in the world. The sun was steadily setting, and the skies seemed all shades of gold. Billy could hear the birds sing, and feel the soft breeze coming in from the ocean. It transported his mind to a state of hallucination where he could perceive the feeling of happiness being surrounded by hundreds of children in his own orphanage. He could also see Margaret helping him, Asha coming and teaching the kids, and John taking over the maintenance responsibility of the place. He visualized his friends coming with a lot of gifts for the kids and spending quality time with them. He could also see Chris come to meet them, and he was extremely proud to see Billy finally doing what he'd always wanted to do. Just then, a hand came from behind and tapped Billy's shoulder.

"Hey, Billy, how is Miami treating you?" Chris was home.

Billy pulled back in astonishment, as if Chris had startled him from a dream.

"Hey, Chris, how are you? So good to see you. Sorry. I was a bit lost in my thoughts and never realized you came in," said Billy.

"Oh nice! It's good to dream and feel your dreams. So how was the surprise and how do you feel here? Are you comfortable with everything?" asked Chris.

"Well, I can't say anything, Chris. My words wouldn't do justice to my feelings," said Billy, and he struggled to get up with his crutches and hug Chris tightly. He softly whispered in Chris's ears in an emotional, shaky voice, "Thank you! Thank you! This is even beyond my craziest dreams."

Chris was touched by the gesture. Chris asked for a coffee and joined Billy.

"What a mesmerizing place, Chris," said Billy. "I was, first of all, unable to absorb the whole idea of an outstation trip, and then the Miami thing happened at the airport, then Ron and then this villa with the ocean view. This was like an overload of my completed wish list," Billy said, speaking, continuously out of breath, yet with a big smile on his face.

"Thank you, Billy. I'm glad you're enjoying your trip and stay. For the next three days, you're under house arrest here," joked Chris.

They kept chatting for a while, and then Chris went to his room to change for a swim. It was 7:30 PM, almost sunset time. Billy went back to his dream world to savor the moment and treasure it forever.

Chris came back in his swimming trunks and dived into the pool. Must be quite a relaxing moment after a long day's work. It was quite a sight to see the sun go down. Billy kept sipping a virgin mojito as the sun was setting, with some Bob Marley music playing in the background. Chris came out of the pool and told Billy that they would meet at the same place at 8:30PM for dinner.

**

Chapter 15

The Why before the Where

Everything comes with a purpose. Those who can find the meaning of the purpose, get the fruit.

8:30PM, Chris came over to the pool and met Billy, who was already waiting for him. The weather was perfect to be outdoors, and they decided to take the table near the bar by the pool. Sam had already made a lovely cabana setup on the lush, green grass to the left of the pool. It was dimly lit and perfectly set for two people.

"Why do you think you're in Miami?" asked Chris.

Billy replied, "I'm not so sure, but I'm guessing you wanted to do a few continuous sessions."

"Yes, you're partially correct. Firstly, I had work here and didn't plan to go back to Chicago this weekend. Then I realized that the next sessions were interlinked and needed to be completed together. So, nothing like you coming here and we do our sessions over the weekend. Also, it will be a fun break for you and will help open your mind to new ideas," Chris said and smiled. "Now that you're here, let's make the best of it. And we will surely not find a better place to have our conversations."

Smith served some soup and bread on the table. He also served a bottle of vintage French white wine and an artisanal cheese platter, candied nuts and olives to go with the wine. That was followed by a few exotic salads and finally the main dish—prawns tossed in Asian sauce, accompanied by char-grilled vegetables and potato wedges. Both didn't opt for any desserts and preferred to continue with their drinks.

Chris wanted to go out for a walk but realized he had to do it alone and asked Billy to take a small break till Chris did two rounds of the villa. While Chris was walking, Billy kept thinking about how lovely the day had been. He had been sending pics and texts to Asha all the time, telling her that this was probably the best day of his life.

Chris decided to sit in the lovely cabana setup on the lawn, and he asked Smith to move their drinks to the cabana. Chris moved on to his regular whisky, and Billy decided to take a small break. Chris started the conversation.

"In our last meeting, we had discussed briefly all the factors to be considered before launching a brand. There are totally eight points to discuss, and we have to stick to our schedule so that we catch up on all of them by Sunday evening. Today, we would do two topics and then Saturday and Sunday three each. Tomorrow evening, I've organized for a small get together for a few friends, so we have to do this during the day itself," Chris said.

"Sounds like a plan. I'm with you," replied Billy.

Chris continued, "Purpose of the brand, the name says it all. Let me start by asking you one important question. What is your perception about brand purpose and brand vision? Do you feel it means the same thing?"

"Yes, I see brand purpose and brand vision are closely related to each other. Actually, it seems like the same to me. But I'm little doubtful, as you're specifically asking this question," Billy said.

"They're not the same at all. It's very important for us to understand their basic difference. Brand purpose is the *why*, and brand vision is the *where*. The purpose of the brand is the reason for the brand to exist, whereas the vision allows you to define where the brand wants to be in a particular period of time. For example, the brand vision can be 'After five years we want to be the best brand in our industry in terms of revenue across the globe.' Your brand vision can be tweaked with time and can also be more than one. However, the brand purpose is always the same and can never change over time. Brand purpose defines the story of the existence of the brand, based on the past, whereas your vision is about the future," said Chris.

Chris added, "Brand purpose is also a preview of what you want to be in the eyes of your customers. It's what the brand stands for and is beyond just profits. Based on your past experience or understanding, you want to bring in a change for a better tomorrow and that's the story behind creating your brand. A powerful brand purpose results in a powerful product or service. Every successful brand has a very strong brand purpose.

"The whole idea of asking you the difference between purpose and vision was to make you have a better understanding. Do you now understand the difference between purpose and vision?" asked Chris.

"Yes, it's clear. However, I would like to ask one question. Does every brand have a purpose?" Billy asked.

Chris said, "Let me reframe your question. You want to know if every brand defines a purpose? Ironically, not all brands define a purpose, because they follow a basic corporate structure of vision and mission. Many brands are ignorant about defining the purpose or they don't feel the importance of a brand purpose. So in this process, the purpose gets lost. Especially if it's a small-scale brand or company, then purpose never gets priority."

"Oh, I got it now. But is that a considerate practice to leave the purpose aside?" asked Billy.

"No, not at all. We all understand that every business should make profits. But many times, the drive to make profit becomes so strong that the brands forget to pay attention to the purpose. Either they don't define it, or even if it's defined, they don't pursue it. Which means that the purpose has no meaning for that brand. This is one of the biggest mistakes any brand can make, and they'll realize it when the brand fails," Chris said.

Chris continued "In my opinion, the purpose is much more important than the vision and the mission statements. The market is very loud and busy with lot of brands doing similar things trying to sell their products at the tops of their voices. Having a brand purpose sets you apart and helps add value to your customers. It also provides clarity in the mind of your employees and helps build the right brand culture."

"Then it makes much more sense to talk about the purpose, rather than what you do, when you speak about your brand," said Billy.

"Absolutely! Whenever you ask anyone what they do, they speak about what their brand or company does, but rarely anybody talks about the story. The world is exhausted with business ideas and what you do may be just one of the things many other people are doing. So the question is, how do you stand out? But when you talk about *the why*, which is your purpose and your story, it takes your answer to the next level. The simplest brands can have the greatest stories, which elevates the brand," Chris said.

"Let me give you a random example. You have a store that sells vegetables. Now either you can say that you sell vegetables, or you can say that, based on a research, you've found that 99 percent of vegetables are filled with chemicals. So you've done further research to identify all organic farmers. And now you aggregate all your vegetables exclusively from these organic farms and then bring them to your store," cited Chris. "Did you realize the difference between having and not having a purpose?"

"Yes, this is so interesting. The purpose glorifies the whole business of selling a very regular commodity like vegetables. Also, the purpose is driving the product, and if the purpose is clear, then I would never buy vegetables from regular farmers," Billy replied.

"Exactly the point I was trying to explain was that once your business starts, you get driven by profits and growth. In that case, if you lose focus on your purpose, then you might end up buying part of your vegetables from regular farmers, which goes against your brand purpose. So eventually your customers will know that not all your vegetables are from organic farms, which will dilute your brand and probably make it fail," added Chris.

"Wow, that was a remarkably simple example that cleared my concept about purpose in and out," Billy confirmed.

Chris concluded, "In fact, many times when you give a comprehensive thought to your purpose, you come out with a better business idea. And this is why I have been telling you that purpose is one of the most important factors for your brand."

Chris got so engrossed in the conversation that he never realized that his drink was over. Smith came over to check if he wanted a repeat, and it was definitely a yes. Billy also ordered his gin and tonic with a lemon wedge served in a wine glass. They got back into the conversation again.

"Let me also give you a real life example so you're more clear about it. Let's talk about Apple as a brand. Apple's purpose is simply 'to empower creative exploration and self-expression.' They are known to 'think differently' and are always 'challenging the status quo.' They've been awarded the most valuable brand in the world eight times! Profits are definitely important to stakeholders, but the brand always empowered creativity and came across as a very strong brand in the eyes of its customers, resulting in a highly successful brand in the long term," said Chris.

"Steve Jobs in his return speech to Apple employees in 1997 said that Apple is not making computer boxes—it's much beyond that. The core value of Apple is that it believes that people with passion can change the world. And people who are crazy enough to think that they can change the world are actually the ones who do it. The market has changed since the inception of Apple, but the purpose cannot change. He wanted to communicate the same to the world. So he decided to create a campaign where they would honor people who dared to change the world, dared to think differently, and they created the 'think-different' campaign. Apple felt that this factor of 'thinking different' touched the souls of people working at Apple. This was probably one of the speeches of the century. It moved people and eventually built an immense trust and reliability on the brand. Apple worked on their purpose, and it's their brand purpose that made them who they are today," Chris said.

"You need to be extremely passionate about your brand to create a coherent brand purpose. It's that persistent drive that pushes you every day to work towards making your brand unique. You need to understand your creed, the bigger dream, what you believe in, what you want your brand to believe in. What is the social ecosystem difference you will bring in? What is that one change you're willing to persistently fight for? It's about your ideology, which never changes with time," said Chris. "Here we are, done with brand purpose, which according to me is *the* most important point to be considered for the existence of your brand. What do you have to say about it, Billy?"

Billy replied, "Exceptional! I wished you could feel the way I'm feeling at this moment. I feel like creating something that can change the world. It's so unbelievably motivating. Now I can relate to the brand purpose and your statement about making a difference to the existing human social ecosystem. It's just marvelous, Chris, and I agree with every single word you said."

It was already 11:45 PM, but both of them knew that they didn't have to worry about time. They had the liberty to go on till whatever time they wanted. They got up from the cabana and started walking towards the pool. For Billy, it was slow and steady, and when they reached the pool, they saw that Smith and Sam were chatting and listening to some Frank Sinatra. Billy thought that this must be Chris's playlist. They refilled their drinks and took a break before starting the next topic.

***

Chapter 16

Bonding and Branding

What the heart is for a human, the product is for a brand.

Chris and Billy refilled their drinks and laid on the lounge chairs by the pool. While lying on the beds, they were captivated by the view of the clear blue sky filled with zillions of stars. It was too dark to see the water, but they could see it near the deck, which was lit up, shimmering and reflecting the lights falling on it. The gentle breeze was creating small ripples on the water.

On a mission, Chris started the conversation. "Now moving on to the second point, *brand description*. Well, I wasn't sure how to name this section. It could've been named just *product*, but I preferred naming it *brand description* because this topic would involve many internal points beyond just the product. It includes many critical factors that contribute heavily in building a successful brand.

"In this section, we'll discuss the following important points that define a brand. Market research, positioning, naming the brand, logo and designing of the logo, vision and mission, brand values, brand identity guide, and product development.

"Every factor is colossal in itself, but we would cover the essential points for each of them so that you're in a strong position to understand the complete process of building a brand. The first six points are ideally executed by a marketing agency or in-house marketing team, whereas the last point is part of the product designing, production, and quality team. You may need to use the services of an external research company to get a proper market research report," said Chris.

Chris continued, "Let's start with market research, which is the first and foremost factor for any brand when it comes to having a comprehensive understanding about the market position for the product or service offered. The result of the market research would be numbers and graphs, which speak the story of the market conforming to your product. This acts as the benchmark that helps define many other factors that need to be implemented as a part of this brand building process. This helps you maintain competitiveness and an upper hand over competitors. It provides important information required to launch a brand like- what the market needs, demand, market size, competitor analysis, growth rate, and even localized targeted analytics and more. The research can always be chiseled to your requirements."

"I would like to understand. Does every brand practice this exercise? Is it a mandatory step to be executed before launching a brand?" asked Billy.

Chris replied, "Many brands, especially the small ones and average-sized startups, never do an extensive market research. They are happy with a high-level market study and believe more in their instincts. Many times, it might even happen that a business model is exactly catered to the requirement of the market, even without doing a market research. Many wise men even say that the most important factor for any business is your inner calling, and hence, many businesses don't make an effort to do extensive market research. But I would strongly recommend you to do a detailed market research. Market research backed with a strong inner calling is a profoundly successful combination."

He continued very firmly. "We have to be very clear about one thing—wherever it's essential to spend money and involve experts, never compromise. Spend that money, it's not an expense but an investment. One thing I can assure you is that your return on that amount would be much more than you can even think of. Many young and new brands make this mistake of cutting corners to reduce on the initial investments. It's very good to do an exercise of efficient fund management, but not at the cost of quality. If you don't have the expertise and you need to hire a market research company or a brand consultant, then there is no other way but to use their services. You might realize later that this small amount of money can save your brand or take your brand a long way.

"Detailed market research will help you get a deeper understanding of your targeted client segment. You'll get to understand what your competitors are doing and how they approach the market. A winner brand can't go out of business at any point in the brand life cycle. Detailed research would enable you to plan your business growth. Most importantly, it will give you a reassurance and confidence before the launch that your inner calling is in sync with what the market needs," added Chris with an air of confidence.

"Yes, of course! Without doing market research, it would be more like shooting in the dark. I guess it's imperative to do an extensive market research for any brand. I got the answer to my question," Billy reaffirmed.

Chris got up from the lounge chair and walked up to the bar. He asked Smith to refill his drink as he sat by the bar and lit a cigarette. Billy also lit one and continued lying on the lounge chair, gazing at the stars. He also checked if the voice notes were being recorded properly and kept his notebook on the side table.

Chris came to Billy and told him, "Let's sit by the water for a while." Billy got up slowly and started walking with Chris with the help of his crutches. There was a wooden deck pathway from the swimming pool, separating both the lawns and going up to where the boat was parked.

Billy's crutches got stuck in one of the gaps between the wooden planks, and he lost balance and fell on his shoulder. Chris immediately got down to help Billy, and Smith came running from the bar. Billy felt embarrassed but got back up on his crutches with a little help from Chris and Smith. He got a tiny scratch on his elbow. Smith cleaned up his wound and put a Band-Aid on it. After this, nobody gave much importance to the fall and kept walking towards the deck.

Chris sat on the deck, dipping his legs in the water, and Billy preferred sitting on the chair nearby. Smith shifted their drinks to the deck and placed them on a coffee table between Chris and Billy.

Chris continued, "Brand positioning, that's our next point in this section. What do you understand by brand positioning Billy?" Chris smiled.

"It helps a brand create an image of a product or service in the minds of its target audience," replied Billy.

"Excellent! That's a short yet great explanation about brand positioning. It's a marketing technique which creates a perception of a product or service amidst its consumers. Based on the market research and the purpose of the brand, you determine the position of the brand in the market. Anybody who is launching a new product or service needs to understand that there is no product that can be targeted for everybody in this world. Which means that every product or service has a targeted clientele and identifying the right segment of crowd is the process of product positioning. You can never make the mistake of trying to market your product to anybody and everybody. That happens when you're not sure about your TG or you forcefully want to have a bigger audience without doing a proper market research exercise. You can have more than one targeted segment—primary and secondary segments. In that case, you have to define the marketing strategies for both the segments," said Chris.

"A brand should never rush through this process, because this is a key factor in making a brand successful. A right product marketed to the wrong consumers can end up a disaster. You should precisely establish where your product fits in the market, what defines your product as an exclusive product, and what image you want to form in the minds of your targeted segment. It communicates to your customers why they should choose you over other competitors," Chris added.

Chris continued, "Always remember one very important point, brand positioning is the base of all marketing stories for a brand. No product can be marketed effectively without a focused target group.

"You can identify your target markets by using the classic method of TAM (total available market), SAM (segmented addressable market), and SOM (share of the market). Your targeting for SAM and SOM would define your success. Many times, it's a good practice to use conventional methods to reach the right decision.

"Let's wind up this point with some examples. BMW always talks about design and technology and never about pricing. Volvo always talks about safety. Tesla talks about environment, long charge, and speed. Apple talks about innovations and thinking differently. Nike talks about winning and honors the greatest sports people. Uber speaks about ease of transportation. And so on. Each and every established brand precisely knows their TG and always keeps their communication consistent," concluded Chris.

While they still enjoyed the calmness of the water and the intensity of the conversation, Chris continued, "The next point of our conversation is brand name. This is one of the toughest things to achieve. Can also be a lot of fun."

"How can this be the toughest? I'm utterly surprised," asked Billy.

"You might take a day or even years to finalize on a brand name. Some of the important points to be remembered while naming your brand are— it should be easy to spell and must sound simple; it should be easy to remember; and you should be able to trademark and register it in all the geographical locations you're planning to expand to. The URL, dot-com, dot-org, et cetera. or whatever is important for you, should be available. So it's not just the name, but there are many technicalities and legalities that you need to clear up before finalizing the brand name. And that is why it's one of the toughest to achieve," Chris replied.

"It would be ideal if you can associate the brand meaning with the brand name. Many great names are founded on your brand promise, brand values, brand positioning, brand philosophy, or defining the key product line. A highly effective brand name is easy to remember and makes a deep impact in the mind of the client. That's the power of a name," said Chris.

"I guess the trademark and register and the availability of the URL should be at the top of the list. Besides that, it's about what name we like. Is there any guideline for finalizing a brand name?" Billy asked.

Chris smiled. "Yes. Perfect. There are no defined guidelines besides what we discussed. Some people even name a brand after their names or surnames, on kids' names, founders' names, product descriptive names, derivatives names to sound different, acronyms, jumbled words, joining words, and the list is endless. Here is where you can be creative. Just be clear about the technical part and go ahead and enjoy the process of finalizing the name as it's very exciting.

"Most importantly, you should like the name. Remember that sometimes it takes time for a name to grow on you. So allow the name some time and then decide whether you want to consider or discard it," added Chris.

"Let me give you one interesting example of a name, before moving to the next topic. Do you know the story behind the name of the most popular furniture brand in the world—IKEA?" Chris asked.

"Sorry, Chris, I have absolutely no clue about the acronym of IKEA. Honestly, they're so popular that I never cared to know. I guess it sounds cool," Billy stated blankly.

"IKEA is an acronym and stands for Ingvar Kamprad Elmtaryd Agunnaryd, where Ingvar Kamprad is the name of the founder, Elmtaryd is the name of the company, and Agunnaryd(A) is the name of his city in Sweden. It's a complicated story for a name, but they are highly successful," said Chris with a smile

That was a brain twister for Billy, as he never expected such an unconventional story behind a highly successful brand that he's heard of all his life.

"The next topic is a quick one. Let's finish that and then head to the bar. I always try to keep myself fresh by changing locations," Chris said, playing with water while moving his legs swiftly.

"Ha-ha, I realized that long ago. I understand the importance of the location to keep your energy levels high. I've been experiencing this from our first session. I also like it that way," said Billy, smiling.

"Tell me, Billy: How important do you think the design of the logo is?" Chris asked.

"I guess it's extremely important. It's the face of the brand. It can talk to customers," said Billy.

"Yes, it's important, so important that it can make a brand as well. Many times, we underestimate the power of a logo. And, hence, this becomes a very important factor for brand description, even more important than the name. The creative brains designing the logo should have a very comprehensive understanding about the brand philosophy. They should know the brand from the founder's eyes and heart. So it becomes extremely essential for the founders or the core team to spend good amount of time with the creative team and do a detailed brand knowledge transfer in forms of discussions or documents," Chris said.

"Oh! I never thought that the logo design would be so important. I always knew that it has to look good, and that's about it," said Billy.

"Not just about looking good, Billy. There are some logos that even narrate the story of the brand. There are some which give a positive vibe about the brand. There are logos that makes people feel exclusive and leave a long-lasting impression in their minds.

"There's so much to a logo. Using the right colors, fonts, size, imagery, just countless things that make the logo. These components together give birth to a new feeling, a new emotion. You know, happiness, warmth, exclusivity, class—these feelings are invoked because of the logo. You get one chance to do it. Do you want to compromise on that?

"That's the power of a strong, well-designed logo. Never compromise on the logo. If you have to do thousands of iterations till you're satisfied, don't hesitate. A logo is not a job to be completed, but your brand's mark and that's what people see and remember," said Chris.

"I totally understand what you're saying. Sorry for my ignorance about such an important factor. Is there any thumb rule for designing a logo?" Billy asked.

"You don't have to be sorry, Billy. You're learning. This is a topic that can go on for the entire day. I'm sure every brand would hire a creative agency or an individual to design the logo. Ideally, they have thorough understanding about the art of logo designing. Whenever I'm helping a brand with their logo, these are the key points I work on. I call it the STDS (simplicity, timeless, depiction, striking) naming philosophy. Also you may not find STDS in Google search as it is my self-made abbreviation," Chris said with a smile.

"Simplicity. This always stays at the top of my list. The most admired logos in the world are always the simplest. It's very important to understand that creating the simplest logo is the most complex ability. It takes a lot to eliminate all thoughts and leave only the essentials. Good examples would be the Nike swoosh, FedEx, Google, IBM.

"Timeless. A logo should sail across time. Many times, you like a logo, but with time, your affinity toward the logo comes down. If you're feeling this way, so will your customers. So the logo design has to be persistent and must always be in tune with times, staying forever young. Some examples would be Sony, Arrow, Apple.

"Depiction. A logo should tell the story or be an illustration of the products or brand name. These type of logos create a forceful connection. It's a good practice if you can achieve this connection, but many brand gurus also say that some part of the brand should be mysterious to your customers. Some examples would be Twitter, Apple, UPS, Target, Woolmark. Some logos also carry beautiful hidden meanings like that of Amazon. Did you know that the yellow arrow that goes from A to Z in the Amazon logo is more than just a decorative swoosh? The message is that they sell everything, and this also represents the smile that customers experience.

"Striking. One more way of looking at the design of a logo is to make it striking. This is not a common practice, but many brands like this style.

This comes with a risk of your customers getting bored of you, if it isn't done right. However, these types of logos help get immediate attention. For instance, the golden arch of McDonald's.

"During the logo finalization process, ensure that you check the logo in both colored and mono version and that both the versions should look equally good. Also design the logo to be scalable. You might have one product today, but later you might increase your product portfolio and hence the logo should be flexible enough to be scaled," added Chris.

It was 12:20 AM, and Chris was on a roll. Who would have known that he'd had a long day at work and that he'd been continuously mentoring Billy since 9:00 PM? Though Billy has been putting his best efforts to learn everything in the best possible way, but still, at times, he felt that Chris could be very intense, sometimes a bit too much to bear, but he enjoyed this intensity anyway. For Billy, it was always amazing to watch Chris and realize how important it was to be passionate in life—so much so that it becomes a habit of successful people in whatever they did. It didn't matter whether they were benefiting from it or not, but the fervor was always the same. Billy admired Chris and his passion for life.

"The night is still young. Let's grab one more drink," said Chris. They got up from the deck and started walking toward the bar. Chris took a chair at the bar and lit his cigarette and started chatting with Smith. Billy sat next to Chris and also lit his cigarette and asked for a repeat.

"Sir, don't you get tired working round the clock?" asked Smith to Chris.

"It's exactly what I was thinking a while ago," Billy said.

Chris smiled. "The thing is, I don't get tired if I'm doing what I like to do. Otherwise, I'm bored in a second. At this moment, I'm enjoying the company, the moment, the weather, being one with nature, and, moreover, mentoring is my passion, so there's no chance that I'll get tired or bored, especially when I'm mentoring the right person."

"So, Mr. Billy, shall we move on to the next topic, or you're tired?" asked Chris.

"Not at all, Chris. How can I be tired when I'm learning what I always wanted to? We can definitely move on to the next point," Billy responded.

"Brand vision and mission can look confusing to new entrepreneurs. Vision is the *where* and mission is the *how*," said Chris.

"Brand vision is the future, the where—where the company wants to be. You can define your short-term vision or long-term vision or both. It's more aspirational and gives a direction to the brand. It can also be tweaked with respect to the time and situation. The most important thing about vision is that it should be measurable," Chris said.

"Brand mission is about today, *how* the company will act today to achieve its brand vision. It's the core of the business and is what you do every day. It includes the strategy, activities, and decisions to be taken on a daily basis to reach the vision. It's the driving force and the route to success for the brand," added Chris.

"Oh wow! That was short, simple, and so well explained. Can you give me a few examples?" Billy said.

"Let's take the example of Tesla. Their brand vision statement is 'to create the most compelling car company of the twenty-first century by driving the world's transition to electric vehicles.' The key words over here are 'most compelling,' 'car company,' 'twenty-first century,' and 'world's transition to electric vehicles.' Their mission statement is 'to accelerate the world's transition to sustainable energy.' So mission is your path to reach the vision," said Chris

"Let me also summaries a very important analogy—purpose is based on the past, vision is the future, and mission is today. If you remember this, then you'll never go wrong," Chris concluded.

"Let me now explain to you one of the core factors, which we call *brand values*," said Chris. "Brand values are the thought line of a brand and stands

at the core of the brand. Many of us look at a brand as a service or a product, but in reality, it's much beyond that. A brand is what you stand for, and it's the brand values that define *who* you are."

"I presume that the brand values are the guiding principles for each and everybody who's internally or externally associated with the brand?" asked Billy.

"Yes, it is. These are the beliefs that a common set of people working in the same brand subscribe to. Your product or your services may change with time, but the brand values remain the same. However, it's equally tough to arrive at your core brand values. You may require some time to understand and define the same. It's very important to set the right core values as that is how a consumer looks at the brand. Many consumers end up buying from the brands where they feel that their core values align with that of the brand," said Chris.

"I completely got the point. How do you arrive at your core brand values?" asked Billy.

"As I said, this is a difficult task. You need to ask yourself what values are important for you and the brand, and make a list. Then you can revisit the list and retain only the important ones. You might get driven by the commonly used, idealized brand values, but that may not be the right approach. The core values are not a display of words but a realistic practice. So if you want your ideologies to stand out and be original, then you have to make a list of values that you are passionate about," said Chris.

"It's also important that your brand should stand up for a cause, and this cause becomes one of your core values. You might look at what value your product and service can bring to the world. You might look out at what your customer would expect from you. You might also look at what your closest competitors are practicing," said Chris.

"Many brands practice the reverse process. They make a list of what they don't want as a part of their values and consider the opposite of that in their list," added Chris.

"Reverse process? That was interesting. What I feel is that even if I do a regular process, the reverse process might help me reach at understanding better core values. Do your brand values change with time?" asked Billy.

"Yes, many brands take the help of the reverse process at times to ensure that they want to retain a particular brand value or not. The negative logic of human beings is much stronger than the positive logic. Like, you may not know why you like something, but you will know why you don't like something. The brand values ideally don't change at all. But at times, you might need a little while to understand and define a few of the values clearly. There might be very small changes to the core values, but the main set of core values don't change," replied Chris.

"This definitely calls for a small break," said Chris with a smile. Billy couldn't second that more. Both took a quick break before getting back to the next point.

"Now that you've done the brand purpose, name, logo, vision and mission, TG, brand value, and more, it's very important to capture the technicalities in a document that acts like a guideline, called the *brand-identity document*. This is the guideline to defining the face of the brand. A comprehensive brand-identity guideline works as an extremely strong tool for the marketing team for all brand communications," said Chris.

"So it's more of a rule book for brand communication?" asked Billy.

"Yes, it is, but it also includes many details about the brand for internal as well as external communications," Chris replied.

"Do we need to define the audience?" asked Billy.

"Excellent question, Billy. A brand-identity guideline should always define its audience like internal, external, and partners/associates. The guidelines for every stakeholder has to be mentioned clearly as a part of the document," replied Chris.

"What would be the content of this document?" asked Billy.

"The basic content would be mainly the purpose of the brand, beliefs, vision statement, mission statement, what the brand does, targeted segment, and any other brand description factors," said Chris.

"Besides this, it should include the logo details, color palette, typography, web design, graphics, motion, data representation, brand standards, brand-standard object design, and anything where you can see your logo. The detailing for all these points in the document would be in a format that speaks about how it should be and shouldn't be used. The logo usage and restrictions have to be very clearly defined. You can't leave the usage of your brand open to anybody," said Chris.

"It defines and maintains standards across all media channels so that your brand image is cohesive and communicates the same message across all platforms, whether it's social media, radio or any other form of video or print," concluded Chris.

"Is it important to define the brand identity guideline document before the brand launch?" asked Billy.

"It's a no-brainer. Much before the launch. How would you even launch the brand without having the communication guideline in place? This is the most essential tool for the marketing team before they start working on any brand. Hope we are on the same page?" asked Chris.

"Yes, absolutely! It's very clear now, and I've also realized the importance of this guide. I'll surely be on it when I create my own brand," Billy replied.

"Congratulations, we're left with just one small topic for the day," said Chris. "Are you happy that the day is finally coming to an end?" asked Chris.

Billy smiled. "Well, I'm happy that I could learn so much in one day, and to be honest, I'm also happy that we're almost done for today. I'm overloaded with information."

Chris ordered for a refill of his drink, and Billy decided to take it easy. Chris was used to this lifestyle, and Billy was a newbie. Chris shared many stories about his projects, where he would continuously work for three-to-five days. But that's how the advertising industry works. Lately, Chris had been trying to work towards a better lifestyle. Reducing his cigarettes was one thing he was struggling with, and it got worse every time he had alcohol. But he told Billy that would be nicotine free from the first of January, the coming year.

"So the last topic is *product development*. As per Wikipedia, in product development, 'the product can be tangible (something physical which one can touch) or intangible (like a service, experience, or belief).' Although there are additional differences between the nature of a product and service, in this topic we will use the term *product*.

"The phase of product development is always a *waterfall model*, which means that you may have to repeat the *concept, design, implementation, verification*, and *analysis* phases in a loop, till you perfect the product as per the need of that time," said Chris.

"This becomes the core of your brand, as eventually everything revolves around the product. We get misguided many times that if you have a strong marketing strategy and funds in place, then the product doesn't matter. Please don't fall into this trap. The brand is about the product, and the moment the product fails, the brand will spiral downward. If it keeps failing again and again, the brand will eventually diminish. So creating a strong product becomes the core of the brand. All research, innovations, and studies should be constantly ongoing towards product development. Today's market is very volatile, and you need to be eminently adaptive. If there is any new brand that creates a better solution for the same product line, then the whole market shifts. So product development is not just a pre-brand-launch activity but a lifelong activity," said Chris.

"Many brands with a bad product, might start off really well because of extensive marketing spends and discounts. But they would surely be a failure in the long term. A brand is never a short-term project, and those who understand the long-term blueprint are the ones who create a brand," added Chris.

"The biggest example would be Nokia. From 1998 to 2007, Nokia dominated the cell phone market. But due to lack of constant innovation and market adaptiveness, they lost all market share. And by 2011, it went down to making losses. Even today, in the list of the top ten ever selling mobile handset models, seven models are recorded in the name of Nokia. When such giant brands can fail due to lack of consistent product development, then it becomes very crucial for a new brand to focus on product development," said Chris.

"Today's buyers are smart, intelligent, and well researched. They have an acceptable understanding about the product quality. And if this fact is respected by a brand, then they are on the right path," summarized Chris.

"The Nokia story has always been unbelievable to me. It's so hard to believe that a colossal brand like Nokia could ever fail. Which can bring doubt to any business model, and at the same time, motivates me to be on my toes in any form of business," said Billy.

"I'm glad you're thinking that way. The only way of thinking is that if you constantly work toward getting the right product, then you will never fail your customers," said Chris.

"So that's it, Billy. We are done for today. Let me be honest, even I'm tired now," laughed Chris with a sense of relief.

"That was quite a lot. My notebook is kind of full today, and I've got all the voice notes as well. It was just one more amazing day with you, Chris. I can never thank you enough. It's not just the mentoring, but the experience you have given me on a personal level is out of this world. I'd lost the hope to live, and today, I'm probably experiencing the best life. I'm living large! And all thanks to you," Billy said with intense gratitude.

"Stop thanking me so much, Billy. Let's just have fun. Rephrasing this—I'm having a great time as well, and I want this to be a fun experience for you. I have faith in you. You're going to do very well for yourself someday, and I can't wait to see that day," replied Chris.

It was almost 2:00 AM, and Chris looked fresh as ever. He was chatting and pulling Smith's leg and asked him to get some fruits. Then suddenly, he got an idea and bounced it off to Billy like a little child excited about Christmas. "Hey, Billy, how about going fishing early in the morning? I can drive the boat, and we can ask Smith to join us. He has a license to drive the boat as well."

For a moment, Billy couldn't believe the energy level of this person. He'd worked from 9:00 AM to 6:00 PM and then been mentoring him from 9:00 PM till 2:00 AM, and now this bundle of energy wanted to go fishing early in the morning. But he let it pass, as he had already experienced examples of Chris's unreal energy levels.

"What is the definition of early morning, Chris, especially when it's already 2:00 AM?" said Billy with a smile.

"Well, I would love to start at 5:00 AM, but considering you have traveled today, let's go at 7:00 AM. What do you say?" asked Chris.

" 7:00 AM would be great," Billy replied.

"Ok then, sounds like a plan. Smith, we'll have breakfast in the boat. Would appreciate if you can arrange that," said Chris.

"So we meet tomorrow, 7:00 AM at the deck," Chris said and departed.

Billy was tired, and he headed toward his room, and in no time, he was fast asleep.

***

Chapter 17

Setup and Infrastructure Planning

Controlled overheads are the umbrella for a rainy day.

Six forty in the morning, Billy got dressed and came near the pool.

"Good morning, Billy, hope you slept well," said Smith, who was dressed in an all Hawaiian get-up with a big hat.

Billy smiled. "Good morning, Smith. Yes, I slept very well. You look funky?"

"Yes, I'm in the Hawaiian mood today. Boats are always fun, especially in the mornings," replied Smith.

When both the boys were chatting, Chris came jogging toward them. "Good morning, Billy, good to see you on time."

"Good morning, Chris, don't tell me you woke up early and went for a run!" said Billy, astonished at first and then realizing that this shouldn't surprise him.

"Yes, I was up at 6:00 AM, which is actually later than my regular time of 5:00 AM. I just finished my morning run and workout. If you can give me fifteen minutes, I'll finish my meditation and join you guys," Chris replied.

"Yes, of course! Please go ahead. We will wait for you at the boat," replied Billy.

Chris had told Billy that meditation was the driving force behind his powerful mind. It helped him reach his inner soul, be controlled and guided. This was his way of enriching his body with positive energy and letting go of all the negatives. According to research, studies had shown that meditation was the most influential life changer for many successful professionals. Routine meditation had a compounding result on one's life. It helped declutter the mind and achieve peace. Chris believed a mind at peace was in its best state to make decisions.

Billy and Smith headed to the deck. Billy was on his crutches, having left his wheelchair in the room. Smith had already prepared everything in the boat, and then he helped Billy board the boat. He also prepared the fishing hooks with some prawn bait. The boat was relatively small in size compared to the one Chris had in Chicago. This one could seat ten-to-twelve people but was remarkably fancy and more lavish. It was white with brown leather seats all over. The pilot cabin also blended in with the fancy setting, owing to a convertible rooftop. There were lounge chairs on the front and the rear of the boat. Anyone would leave a bigger yacht to be in this lavish boat. It was like leaving a SUV to drive a fancy convertible.

"Have you sailed this one before, Smith?" asked Billy.

"Yes, many times, but never in Miami," Smith replied.

7:00 AM sharp, Chris came over to the deck in his jogging shorts, "Are we ready to go Smith?" he asked. He hopped into the boat and made himself comfortable on one of the chairs at the back end. Smith offered some juice to both Billy and Chris and started the boat. He took the boat deep into the ocean, passing through shallow currents and the waves hitting the boards of the boat and finally stopped when they arrived in still, deep-blue waters where they could see some a few more boats parked to fish. They took out their fishing rods, and Smith helped them with the prawn bait. Chris looked like a pro, though Billy was not so bad for a first timer. Smith got busy with making breakfast, and he started spreading it out on the front deck, where there was more seating to lounge around in. He had prepared some grilled chicken sandwiches and served them with cold meats, fruits, and nuts. Both Chris and Billy placed their fishing rods in the holders on the railing of the boat and shifted to the front part of the yacht for breakfast. Chris never made Billy feel that he was giving him special attention or helping him because he was physically challenged. He always left Billy to himself but also made sure that he was doing fine. Smith went to the rear of the boat to keep a watch on the hooks, carrying his sandwich with him. Both Chris and Billy wore their fishing hats as the sun was getting strong.

"Hope you slept well, Billy," asked Chris.

"Yes, Chris. I crashed immediately after you left, and I slept like a baby. It was tiring but one of my best days ever," said Billy, smiling.

"I'm glad you're enjoying the trip. There's more to come. Let's get to our work. This evening we won't have any time. We need to finish all the three points during the day itself."

"Yes, I'm ready to start," replied Billy

"Great! Today's first point of discussion is setup and infrastructure planning," said Chris.

They continued their conversation while they were having their breakfast.

"The business setup and infrastructure plan is the core for setting up any business. Many companies include these details in the overall business model. However, I recommend you do this separately, right at the start, as this can be quick and handy. It can later merge and become a part of the business-plan document. The role of this document is extremely important to find the first hand feasibility of the business. It includes comprehensive details about the capital requirements for setting up a business and enabling it to run for a minimum of six months," said Chris.

"This plan has three components—people, operations, and processes. You should ideally create a plan for all the three components independently. Some brands use the terms *basic physical*, which maps the *operations; organizational*, which maps the people; and *services and facilities*, which mostly maps processes," said Chris.

"Interesting! So how do you go about the planning before setting up the business?" asked Billy.

Chris started moving from the lounge and walked up to the rear end to continue fishing. Billy followed.

"You can't start any business without doing the business setup and infrastructure planning. Many times, businesses don't plan their available capital and investment required. That is why one might start setting up a business and get stuck before launching or during the first few months of operations. As a result, you're unable to launch the business, and at the same time your monthly operational costs trigger, pushing you into deeper problems. On one hand, you're trying to arrange funds to complete the setup and launch. On the other hand, you're also struggling to meet your regular operational cost. So this becomes a vicious cycle, which is very difficult to come out from," Chris replied.

"Oh! This can be really bothersome. So what should be the ideal way of planning your setup and infrastructure cost?" asked Billy.

"We need to be very realistic in launching a brand. This is one segment where optimism doesn't help. We need to have a very clear understanding about the current cash in hand or the cash flow in due course of time to set up the brand. Once you have the precise numbers, you need to start working on two components—setup cost and the operational cost for at least six months. At the end of this exercise, you would be able to gauge the feasibility of this particular business under careful consideration," said Chris.

"And when you have enough capital to invest, it can also be the other way round, right?" asked Billy.

"Yes, in that case, you freeze on the business and then calculate the setup and infrastructure cost. Based on the final numbers, you arrange for the capital. This is fine when you have enough capital in hand. When you have a limited capital, then it's always better to follow the other method, where you work out your plan based on the capital. You might sometime realize that this business is not viable with the available capital, which is better than getting stuck midway," said Chris.

"But ideally, do the complete setup and infrastructure planning first, and based on that, you do the financial planning to start the business. You might be able to define stages to break the cost, which will help you keep the initial cost lower," continued Chris.

Suddenly, Billy's fishing rod started moving. Billy got excited and started reeling his rod. "Looks like a big one. Keep reeling," commented Chris. Billy kept reeling until he saw a big fish head come out of the water. He was super excited to see his catch. Chris helped him pull it up to the boat. It was an amberjack, which would easily weigh around forty pounds.

"That's a big catch, Billy," Smith shouted from the other end of the boat and looked very excited.

"I guess you got lunch for all of us. We don't need any more. This is what I call beginner's luck," said Chris.

Billy had caught many fish before, but this would be his biggest ever. He was extremely proud of himself, and somehow he got a superstitious feeling that maybe things are changing for the better for him. Chris and Billy got back to their conversation immediately after Smith came forward and helped unhook the fish.

"What are the factors to be considered while estimating the setup cost?" asked Billy

"Some of the common factors can be real estate (purchases or rentals and deposits) for office/retail/warehouse/factory, setup and interior cost for the same, licensing and permits, legal and insurance, equipment and supplies, market research, employees' salaries, inventories, utilities, marketing and sales, online and physical marketing materials. The cost associated with each component can be in part or full before the launch, depending on the nature of business. Based on that, if you put the numbers against all the components, you'll arrive at the total setup cost," replied Chris.

"Besides the setup cost, we need to estimate the infrastructure/operational cost as well, right?" asked Billy.

"Yes, that's the next step. You need to consider what are your operational costs per month for the upcoming year. To define your cash on hand before the launch, you need to consider the operational cost for at least six months. The operational cost is the cost incurred to operate a particular business. It includes the cost of all resources used by an organization just to maintain its existence. Operational cost is of two types—variable operational cost and fixed operational cost," Chris replied.

"The fixed operational cost is cost that needs to be incurred irrespective of the business status. Some of the common fixed operational cost components are rentals, EMIs, employees' salaries, sales and marketing activities, research, maintenance, travel and transportation, and basic daily expenses," added Chris.

Chris continued. "The variable operational cost depends on the sales and how it has been operated. Some of the common variable cost components would be raw materials, products, services, maintenance, travel and transportation and basic daily expenses. Some of the components appear in both the cost types – fixed and variable costs."

By this time, Billy was completely confused and forgot about his excitement of catching a big fish. He wanted to clarify few important things, which Chris realized and gave him time to understand the topic better. Even though Billy was recording all the voice notes, he preferred asking his doubts on the spot instead of waiting for later.

Chris moved toward the steering wheel and decided to take control for some time. They pulled up their rods and started the boat toward an island. Just before reaching the island, Chris stopped the boat and anchored it. He asked Smith to take out the snorkeling gear. He put on his equipment and dived into the water. Before diving, he asked Billy to wear his snorkeling gear and take the support of the ladder so he could snorkel in the same spot. Billy was a little hesitant, not sure whether he could do it or not. But both Chris and Smith helped him get down from the boat, and he stayed in the water while he held on to the ladder. He went into the water with his snorkeling gear, mesmerized by the gorgeous view under the surface. There were beautiful kinds of fish in all colors, shimmering corals, and water plants mixed with stones. He got lost in the prodigious beauty of the ocean. He wished that he could stop time and experience this amazing feeling forever.

They continued snorkeling for half hour more, and then Chris took the boat around the island to show Billy the alluring beauty, they then headed back to the next fishing spot. He parked the boat, gave the controls to Smith, and went back fishing. He also asked Smith to help them with some beer. Billy was still lost in the dreamy world of the mysterious ocean.

Chris wasn't so lucky that day and caught only two small fish. Billy added three more small fish to his bucket. Then Chris asked Smith to take the boat back to the villa. Chris went back to their conversation as they were almost reaching the deck.

"So, Billy, what more do you want to know about this topic?" asked Chris.

"I wanted to know how do you finally arrive at the capital requirement. I got the point that we have the setup cost, we have the fixed cost and the variable cost, and all this will add up to our required investment for the business. If you could tell me some basic thumb rule to arrive at the number, then I'll have a better understanding," said Billy.

"To arrive at your investment cost, you have the setup cost, which we understand. On top of that, you need to arrive at an operational cost month on month for the first year, including your fixed cost and tentative variable cost. Ideally, you need to consider at least six months of operational cost for a small-scale business. Then you add the setup cost and the operational cost for six months and arrive at the investment required to launch that brand," said Chris.

Investment Required = Setup Cost + Operational Cost for six months (Fixed + Variable)

"The important point of caution over here is to never be optimistic while making your investment sheet. Always keep some buffer and be as detailed as possible so that you don't run out of cash before launching the project," said Chris.

"Also, you need to work under a precise and controlled operating cost environment. Lavish spending is not the call of the hour, unless and until you have very strong capital in hand. You can always upgrade your standard of operations with time. An incremental model is the safest mode to grow a company, mostly for new entrepreneurs. The success of the business is more important than your personal liking. So it's my advice, never to get emotional while spending and stick to the basic investment model," said Chris.

"Yes, got the point. Every factor you discuss sounds like the most important factor to be considered and detailed out before launching the brand. I'm amazed to know how much detailing goes on paper even before launching a brand," said Billy, amazed.

"Yes, it does. And those who do it the right way are the ones who stand a better chance at launching a successful brand. It's always better to create a comprehensive structure for your business model and work on your prelaunch activities. Never compromise on this phase as this decides the fate of your brand," said Chris with a lot of tenacity.

They reached the villa at 11:10 AM and sat in the living room. Sam served them some chilled water and lemon juice to revive their energy. Chris decided to take a small break and then the plan was to meet at the pool by 11:45 AM. Billy also went into his room and got fresh and changed into his pool shorts.

***

Chapter 18

Distribution Channels

The process of building a brand is like a relay race. The brand, the distribution partner, the sales partner work as one force to establish brand success.

Billy took a quick twenty-minute power nap and was rejuvenated. Chris finished some calls in the meantime and dived into the pool. Billy had to change into his swimming shorts, as they were going into the pool. He now took a little extra time when it came to getting himself changed because of his leg. Life, all of a sudden, had changed for him, and he was still getting used to the new way of doing things. He joined Chris in the pool and Smith served them some chilled fresh watermelon mojito.

Chris took the first sip and said, "Heavens! This drink is so fresh and good, Smith."

"Thank you, sir," replied Smith, smiling. Chris and Smith went a long way back. Chris helped Smith many times with many things, and Smith has always been faithful to Chris and goes everywhere he goes. Making Chris happy made Smith happy.

Billy hadn't yet started swimming after the accident. So he waited in the water by the drinks and kept enjoying his mojito. Chris went for few laps and then came over to his drink.

"So what's the topic now, Billy?" asked Chris.

Billy was prepared and replied, "Know and reach your target group—your TG."

"What do you understand from this line?" asked Chris.

"We have to understand who our product and service caters to. We have already done that in the brand-definition part. Once we are aware of our TG, then we need to find the right *distribution channel* to reach out to our customers," Billy replied.

Chris smiled, feeling a good sense of satisfaction, just the way a teacher felt when his students understood the subject. "Very true, Billy, I guess you have been following my notes well."

"Now that we have a basic understanding about the concept, let's discuss a few details. Once we have created the product, we need to define a method of making our product available to the targeted end customer, which is the distribution channel. It's important for us to understand all the stakeholders in this cycle starting from the production team to the selling team. The four main stakeholders are manufacturers, distributors, retailers, and customers," said Chris.

"The channel of making our products reach the customers can be direct or indirect. Some of the direct channels are self-owned stores, internet, sales teams, catalogues. Some indirect channels are wholesalers, distributors, franchisees, resellers, dealers, retailers, and agents," said Chris

"I can understand the direct-distribution model. Would love to know more about the indirect distribution model?" asked Billy.

"The most prominent indirect distribution models are franchises and dealerships," replied Chris.

"Franchisees are exclusive sales partners for the brand, and they're a replica of the brand's own store. Under this model, the whole process of manufacturing and product development is in the scope of the brand. Setting up the store, sales, and service are in the scope of the franchise partner. This is the best model for rapid growth; as the brand can streamline its investments and focus on the products and processes and the partners can focus on the store. This model also creates a focused area of expertise for both the stakeholders," said Chris.

"Is the business relationship exclusive with each other?" inquired Billy.

"The store mostly deals exclusively with the brand's product line. There may be a few exceptions, but these are generally very rare. But some brands do follow an exclusive franchise model for a certain location, and some follow a hybrid of direct selling and franchise selling or exclusive product lines from the same brand. That purely depends on the policy of the brand. Most successful franchise brands work on a two-way exclusive model," Chris replied.

"So it's always a direct relation between the brand and the franchise partner?" asked Billy.

"For the ease of your understanding, let me explain one more term related to this part of the topic. Franchisor is the company or the brand that allows an individual or another company to run a location of their business. In case of a direct franchise between the brand and the franchisee, then the brand is a franchisor. The brand can also allocate and appoint a franchisor, who would appoint franchisees on behalf of the brand. In that case, the franchisor is not the brand but is one more party appointed by the brand.

"So, in some cases, you also have a franchisor who interacts directly with the brand and allocates and appoints franchisees on behalf of the brand. In this case, the brand doesn't get involved in allocating franchisees in the defined area for the franchisor. Setup and operations for those stores can be direct or indirect between brand and the franchisees, depending on the brand policy," replied Chris.

"Sorry, this sounds very important to me, and I have lots of questions. How do you handle operations for this model?" asked Billy.

"The standards and processes of setting up the store, executing sales, operations, and the service policy is strictly defined by the brand. The franchise partner, his team, and the store is the face of the brand and, hence, an integral part of the system. In reality, it's a partnership, where the brand joins hands with a like-minded professional. This model is tightly coupled, and this model can be made successful only when the brand ensures that each and every partner is capable of being an intrinsic part of the brand culture and process. The brand should also ensure that the store is considered a partner and not an external entity. The brand should also have a strong support system in place to assist the partner in setting up business as well as daily operations. The brand also needs to have constant checks and processes in place to secure brand value," Chris replied.

"In this model, you have to ensure that your processes and communications are very well documented. The same needs to be trained and educated to the teams in the store. The core of this model is scalability, and you can do so only when your processes are scalable," added Chris.

"That makes lot of sense. As always, can you please give me an example?" said Billy.

"McDonald's, as I mentioned, is the biggest example for a franchise model. Every store of McDonald's would look the same, the food would taste the same. Even the internal processes of operations would be same for each and every store. So the brand has defined templates and processes that are executed exactly the same way in all the outlets," said Chris.

"There is no problem with this model?" asked Billy.

"Choose this model only when you have a heart big enough heart to share your brand with partners. Choose the right partners and support this model with stringent processes and a regular training process. Only then, you won't face issues. Smaller problems will always be there in any business model, which you don't really have to worry about," replied Chris.

"Let me also explain to you the dealership model. In this model, the brand grants a license or authorization to a single or multiple-brand retail store. Dealers buy their products from the distributor or brand and sell them to the end customer. The mode of operation is as per the dealer store policy," added Chris.

"In the franchise model, the brand and the partner business relationship is very tightly coupled. Is it the same for the dealer model also?" asked Billy.

"The dealer model is comparatively less coupled, and the relationship is more like a buyer and a seller. There isn't much interaction on daily operations between both the stakeholders. All that matters end of the year are the sales volumes. If the dealer isn't doing good sales, either he will end the relationship with the brand, thinking the brand isn't working for him, or the brand would leave that dealer, thinking the dealer is unable to do justice to the brand. This is an ideal model for a product to start selling immediately as the same line of products are already present in the same store and there is an existing clientele," Chris replied.

"Sony would be a great example. They may be an exclusive store or co-exist with other similar product lines. All that matters to the dealer and the brand is that sales are happening," said Chris.

"Since so many stakeholders are involved in both the models, there's a high possibility of the brand value getting impacted. How do you handle that?" asked Billy.

"Yes, many times when the brand isn't directly selling, then the brand value could be at risk, especially when the franchisee or dealer isn't efficient or isn't following processes and standards. It's very important to protect the brand by having very stringent policies that need to be followed by all the stores. Also, it's important to maintain a healthy relationship with the dealers or franchise partner, as both are working towards the same goal of doing better sales. It's one of the toughest business models, especially the franchise model," said Chris.

Chris came out of the pool and went to the BBQ area, where Smith had prepared lamb chops and mushrooms.

"Smith, please serve me some. I'm starving," said Chris.

Smith served them the best pieces.

"Why do you think people should opt for a franchise or a dealer model?" asked Billy.

"The advantage of the dealer model for the stores is that they can ride on the brand value from the first day. Some of the benefits of the franchise model are that the brand is known, experienced in creating great products and has a ready-to-use business model, all marketing offline and online collaterals are readily available, there is complete support in setting up the business, and constant aid in operations. Whereas building a brand from scratch isn't everybody's cup of tea. If you're sure that you're not a great brand builder, however you're good at sales, then franchise is the ideal model for you," said Chris.

"So the distribution model is a big influencer for your core business model. All brand policies, pricing, guidelines, and strategies would be based on the distribution model," added Chris.

It was already 1:45 PM, and Smith served some main dishes to Chris and Billy. He had prepared fresh grilled fish in lemon sauce, served with some char-grilled vegetables and baby potatoes. It was the catch of the morning. The fish was extremely fresh and was cooked really well that it melted in their mouths. Post lunch they went to their respective rooms to get some rest and decided to meet at 5:00 PM on the lawn. The evening party was scheduled for nine.

***

Chapter 19

The Chicken-and-Egg Story

A well-written and well-narrated story is always promising. For a brand, the marketing team writes, and the sales team narrates.

At 5:00 PM, Billy came out to the lawn. Chris was already sitting in the cabana with a cigarette in one hand, a book in the other, and a green smoothie on the table. He was in his Hawaiian shorts, black shooter shirt, flip-flops, and his favorite aviators.

"Hello, Chris, good to see you fresh and early," said Billy.

"Hey, Billy, you look fresh. I crashed for some time and woke up early and decided to continue with my book. I love sitting in this cabana and reading whenever I'm alone here," replied Chris.

"Did you get any sleep?" asked Chris.

"Yes, I did. In fact, I slept really well. Feel rejuvenated," Billy replied, smiling. "What's the drink you're having?"

"Oh! This is an avocado smoothie. Do you want one? It's really nice. I guess you should try it," said Chris.

Billy ordered for an avocado smoothie, and Smith got it as soon as he could. As expected, it was cold and nice. Billy said, "Smith never fails to impress me. A never-say-no guy. He must be very happy working for you. He's always wearing a smile and happy to help."

"How is Miami treating you, Billy?" asked Chris.

"Well, Chris, as I said, this is probably my best trip ever and for sure, I'll never forget it my whole life. It's not just about the grandeur of the trip, but the amount of wisdom acquired from you is outstanding. My recorder is my most treasured object right now," said Billy with a smile.

Everybody loves to hear good things about themselves, and so did Chris. He smiled, delighted that Billy was having a great time. Somewhere deep inside his mind, he would've done this not just as a mentor but as a good human being who believed in sharing happiness with people.

"We did good today. We've already finished two topics, and we're going to start the third one, and then we're done for the day. The next topic is a very popular one, sales and marketing strategies," said Chris.

"Do you understand the difference between them, sales and marketing strategies?" asked Chris.

Billy played it safe. "I'm always confused between both the terms. They sound like twins to me. I'd rather not try answering this and leave it to you to explain."

With refreshed energy, Chris started, "A marketing strategy is the detailed plan to create brand awareness to its targeted crowd, build brand loyalty, and align the growth of the brand to its vision. Whereas the sales strategy gets triggered only after the marketing strategy is in place. It's a strategic plan to ensure that the brand sells its products and meets its expected annual turnover." Chris smiled. "So that's the basic difference between both the twins."

"Yes, for sure, now I know which one is which," said Billy, smiling right back at Chris. "How comprehensive are these strategies for marketing and sales before the launch?"

"Let me consider them separately for the ease of your understanding. Marketing strategies should be very comprehensive before the launch of the brand. In fact, the marketing team is one of the busiest teams during that time. They would need to design the logo, the brand identity guideline document, prepare all content, website, print and online promotional content, catalogues, brand profile, all artwork, promotional creatives, product and service videos, testimonials and promotional videos, brand film, stationery design, and a complete strategic plan for the whole year.

Besides this, they also need to plan the grand launch of the brand. A very well-designed launch can help a brand take off immediately. That's a lot of work, and that's what my company does for our clients," said Chris.

"I just mentioned the names of the activities; each and every activity is a mammoth job in itself! And before the brand launch, it's either a new in-house team or a new agency and hence a lot of time also goes into explaining the core of the brand to them. So the marketing team is at its pinnacle before the launch of the brand," added Chris.

"Is there a sequence of activities that the marketing team needs to follow before the launch?" asked Billy.

"Well, many activities overlap and run parallel between the strategy, content, and creative teams. However, a significant sequence can be logo design followed by the brand-identity guideline document. Once the brand-identity document is ready, it becomes the base for all other activities. Then the copy team needs to create all the content. Post that, all the activities can start simultaneously, considering the inter-team dependencies," said Chris.

"I could've never imagined the magnitude of work for the marketing team before the launch. Today, I salute all the marketing teams and agencies, who are always behind the scene, and they do such an amazing job in building the core and launching the brand," said Billy.

"Coming back to your previous question, how comprehensive should the sales strategies be before launch? You can start working on the sales strategies only after the marketing strategy is in place. I have always believed that sales is an art, and it's very important to have a great team that's a mix of experienced and fresh professionals with high energy levels to break into the market. The initial sales strategies would focus primarily on acquiring product knowledge and a lot of team training sessions. It would also include a thorough competitor analysis at the ground level. A good sales team has a deep insight about the brand values, brand beliefs, brand goals, purpose, mission statement, and vision statement," said Chris.

"The sales strategies would primarily include the annual targets and a tentative road map to reach these targets. The sales team is the face of the brand, and they should be the spearheads in exhibiting the highest level of brand culture and discipline. Every company has a distinctive way of selling their products, and it's very important for the management to make the same transparent to the sales team," said Chris.

"I completely agree with you, Chris. Sales is an art, and there's a lot that goes into learning this skill. In fact, they always live with the pressure of ensuring that the brand is performing. If sales fail, then the roots of the brand get shaken," said Billy

It was 6:00 PM, and Billy could see that Smith and Sam were working hard on preparing for the evening party. They were setting the bar and the BBQ. Billy had no clue about it, but he decided to wait and watch. Chris asked for two coffees and lit a cigarette. Billy also lit his cigarette and continued gazing at the water. He could see many boats coming back, birds starting to fly back home and the captivating blue sky where the sun was getting ready to set.

"It looks like both the sales and marketing teams have to work very closely for the success of the brand. How does that work?" asked Billy.

"That's the irony." Chris smiled. "Ideally, they need to work closely for the success of the brand, but in most cases, there is always a tussle between both the teams. It goes to the point of one blaming the other for any form of failure. But I'm glad to see that the new-age companies are building a culture where different teams coexist with harmony, and they prefer working together than having a hard time at work. Yes, both the teams are strongly coupled and need to work very tightly together. The relationship between both the teams is more about planning, executing, reviewing, and analyzing, repeated in loop. Also, one of the prime responsibilities of the marketing team is to ensure that it generates adequate leads for the sales team. The sales team would then work on those leads for closure. This process of lead generation is a key contributor in today's competitive world and needs to be executed with utmost importance. Those brands that have a strong bond between the sales and marketing team and work in a cohesive mode are able to scale the business faster," said Chris.

"During the period of preparing for the brand launch, the management has a very critical role to execute. They need to be actively involved in creating the marketing and sales strategies to ensure that the teams are in sync with the vision of the brand. It's also important for the management to set the right culture between both the teams and ensure that they have regular official meetings and work together as one team toward achieving one goal," added Chris.

"Sorry I'm asking too many questions, but I wanted to know a little more in detail about the marketing plan," asked Billy.

"That's absolutely fine, Billy. You should be asking questions. Otherwise, it gets boring for me. Well, the marketing space is rapidly changing with time. One needs to be very adaptive and open to new ideas and channels. Nowadays, digital media plays a more vital role than traditional media, and hence, you have to evaluate all available options. The marketing plan would include a budget for the year to start off with, the various media channels it would be using over the year, and the composition of budget allocated to each channel. The plan would also include details of campaigns across the year. Once the campaigns are launched, there might be changes based on feedback from the sales teams. However, the tone of communication remains the same," replied Chris.

"One common problem that many small-scale brands face is that they don't define the marketing budget before the launch of the brand, and slowly, they want to link it to sales. However, this becomes a chicken-and-egg situation, where marketing would wait for sales to happen, and sales would wait for marketing to happen. In this kind of situation, the brand growth suffers. So ensure that your marketing budget for the year is defined before the launch of the brand, irrespective of the turnover," cautioned Chris.

"I would also like to inform you about one more very common mistake. If the marketing budget isn't clearly defined, then many brands get attracted to keep profits aside. They start treating the marketing spend as an expense, but it's very important to understand that marketing spends are an investment and not an expense. And this is essential for the brand's growth and existence. You have to persistently focus on the bigger goals of the brand, rather than looking at profits from the beginning," said Chris.

"I guess now you have a fair idea about how the sales and marketing strategies work. As I mentioned earlier, every topic we're discussing can be a book by itself. This knowledge would enable you to be a part of any discussion and understand the flow and sequence of actions. It's more important to have a holistic understanding. For any special topic where you need more information, you can always check on the internet," said Chris.

"I guess I'm good. There was lot of information in this topic. And as you said, I'll start exploring more," Billy replied.

Chris got up from his chair, took off his flip-flops, and started walking on the grass with a cigarette in his hand. He looked relaxed, as they were done with all the sessions for the day. He was looking forward to meeting his friends in the evening.

Billy was also feeling happy about the fact that he was done for the day. He normally liked to take it slow, but there had been a lot of information flowing in the past two days. So he had been focusing hard to keep up with the pace. Sometimes, even if one eagerly waiting to learn and gets flooded with too much information, the brain experiences fatigue and stops functioning. But overall, the day had been good fun, and Billy couldn't forget that he'd caught his biggest fish ever.

Chris came back to the cabana and announced, "My guests will start coming at 9:00 PM. Please join the party. It's nothing official, just a social evening with a few friends."

"I would love to," replied Billy excitedly.

"Is there any dress code for the evening Chris?" asked Billy.

"Not really. But it's people from the fashion industry, so they would be in semi-formals I guess. But don't bother. Just wear whatever you want. It's absolutely fine," Chris replied.

***

Chapter 20

To Socialize or Not to Socialize

A social relationship is an essential part of entrepreneurship until it becomes a personal pain.

This topic is highly controversial. So, really, how important is socializing for an entrepreneur? Wise men say that socializing is the key to success for any business. But not everybody will agree with this. It's a completely personal decision and left up to you. If socialization comes naturally to you, then you're gifted, and it would help your business to a great extent.

But if you're shy by nature and don't believe in socializing, in my opinion, that's fine as well. Eventually it's your brand that will speak. You might miss out on a few opportunities, but that's not the end of the world. A good product will evolve and eventually reach where it has to reach. So if you're someone who believes in spending quality time with your close friends or family rather than socializing with people whom you're not so comfortable with, it's absolutely fine. You must do what makes you feel happy.

In most cases, you simply can't say that you won't socialize at all, this may be harmful for your brand. You have to strike a balance and attend to what's necessary. What's important is that whenever you meet people socially, you have to come across as a humble, transparent, and friendly person. People like to associate with easy people.

However, you should always remember one important point. You're not just socializing; you're also using an opportunity to become a better professional. You'll meet numerous people from various backgrounds and expertise, and there will be a few people with whom you'll have a great connection and would like to spend time with. In most cases, you'll have rich and informative conversations, resulting in a great learning process. This should be motivating enough for you to socialize. We should always keep looking for avenues to share our knowledge and for continuous growth. It's good to go out, see what the world is doing, see what people are considering. In the end, you'll decide what you want to consider and what you want to discard.

It was almost 9:00 PM, and Billy came out of his room. He was dressed in blue jeans and a black shirt to play it safe. He decided to be in his crutches instead of the wheel chair. The guests hadn't arrived yet, and Chris was waiting by the pool. Chris customarily was dressed in black jeans, a black shirt, and blue pair of shoes. He managed to look good in almost everything he wore. Maybe it came naturally to him. Smith, Tom, and Sam had made the bar and got the BBQ ready for the evening.

"Hello, Chris, how's it going?" asked Billy.

"Good, Billy, just catching up on a few emails while I'm waiting for everybody to come in. Let's ask for a drink. We deserve it after such a long conversation today," said Chris, smiling.

Billy smiled back as if acknowledging that statement. Chris ordered for his scotch, and Billy ordered for his regular gin and tonic. They sat by the table, and Chris continued with his emails. Billy was sipping on his drink and taking in the alluring view. Billy got up from the table and went up to Tom and checked on the BBQ. He was glad to see his fish as part of the menu. Tom also prepared king-sized prawns and some chicken for BBQ. There were some luscious-looking cheese-and-nut platters as well.

People started coming on time, and by 9:15 PM, almost everybody had reached the villa. There were around twenty people, out of which very few were from Chris's office, and the remaining were his friends from the modeling agencies. They were a bunch of chilled-out people. Everyone was mostly well dressed. You could see that people made an effort to look their best. Chris introduced Billy to most of the people. Billy also started socializing with them as he was enjoying the ambience. Chris had specially instructed to play deep, melodic house tunes to keep the mood happy and light. The BBQ seemed to be everybody's favorite place, lots of them gathered around to grab a bite. Even the bar started getting busy. Added to this, the splendor of the party was the location which was simply mind blowing and created the right vibe for a Saturday evening. As the evening passed, everybody got into the groove.

Billy came across someone standing by himself, watching the others. Drawn to him, Billy introduced himself and the man did likewise. His name was Steven.

"What do you do, Billy?" asked Steven.

"Well, where do I start? Let's see. I dropped out of college last year, had a major accident where I almost died, and the doctors had to amputate my leg to save me. After that, I almost lost hope of living, went into depression, and then suddenly one day, I realized something. I had a strong feeling that I'm not going to die before I do something meaningful in this second life of mine. This was my truth, like an inner calling you know. And luckily, just then I met Chris. I asked him for help and advice, and now he's mentoring me. I'll soon be an entrepreneur just like Chris. I'll start my own business. Chris has been extremely kind to me, beyond my imagination," replied Billy.

"Quite an interesting story. I'm sorry you had to go through so much. I like your fighter spirit, though, and I'm sure you'll do just great," said Steven.

"Thank you, Steven. Yes, I'll do something big. I've got the same feeling. I'm determined and motivated," said Billy, smiling. "What do you do, Steven?"

"I'm an ad director by profession. I've also directed many short films. In fact, I work a lot with Chris, for many of his clients, and that's how we know each other so well. And, yes, I love my job. It comes with a new challenge every single day," said Steven excitedly.

"That sounds really fascinating. I'm sure you enjoy you work. It shows in the positive aura that you carry," said Billy.

"What business are you planning to start?" asked Steven.

"Well, to be honest, I don't have a business plan in place. But I thought it would be a good idea to learn how to set up a business first and then decide what I want to do. One thing I know is that I'll only do something when I fall in love with the idea. Otherwise, I'll wait. I'm having some great sessions with Chris, and the amount of knowledge I'm acquiring by being with him is unexplainable. Also, I'm sure this knowledge will give me a great direction in terms of doing the right kind of business," Billy replied. "It's actually very funny that I don't even have a business plan in place, and I already feel like I would be successful, ha-ha." Billy laughed.

"I guess that's why Chris agreed to mentor you. As far as I know, he is very selective about where he is investing his time. After all he is a busy guy, right! Now I see why he chose you to mentor. That's the right way to think Billy. And if you hold on to this spirit, then there's no way you would not do well for yourself," said Steven.

Steven added, "We should believe in our dreams and goals and start living our dreams every single day of our life. Write them down in a place where we can see them every day. Wake up in the morning and read these dreams and goals. Do this before sleeping or anytime you're free during the day. When you start believing in them, then there's no way they won't come true."

"Thank you, Steven, for your kind words and for sharing your thoughts. I really appreciate that," Billy said.

"What we are is what we think we are. What we would be is what we think we would be. So it's we who define ourselves," said Steven with lot of assurance, sounding a little like a yogi who'd lived through various eras, imparting this kind of knowledge.

His words pierced straight into Billy's heart, and Billy felt enlightened. He looked into Steven's eyes and acknowledged and thanked him, and Steven reciprocated. They continued their conversation for some more time where it became more heartfelt, and Billy shared the idea of his ultimate goal to open an organization like We Care, which Steven really appreciated. They got extremely friendly. Steven gave Billy his card and said he could call him if he needed any help, anytime, and he would be glad to chip in. Billy exhibited honesty, humbleness, and the power to connect to people's hearts—qualities one must aspire to have in order to reach where one dreams to reach.

It was a great experience for Billy, meeting so many talented and high-spirited people. They were full of life and doing what they loved to do. Billy met quite a lot of people, had interesting conversations with them, felt motivated, and most importantly felt a great change.

The party went on till midnight, but Billy decided to call it a night. He had been having long days continuously and more awaited him in the future as well. Billy found Chris sitting among his friends, and wished him good night and thanked him for the party.

Chris told him to take it easy in the morning and that they would meet for breakfast at 8:00 AM.

**

Chapter 21

Know Everything Inside Out

If heaven is your goal, then planning to get there is the stairway to heaven. – inspired by Led Zeppelin

"Good morning, Billy, did you sleep well?" asked Chris, who was already in the living room and enjoying his morning coffee with all the glass doors collapsed, opening up the space of the living room and making it a part of the pool deck.

"Good morning, Chris, great party yesterday! I had good fun and met many wonderful people. Also, I slept really well. I guess I was very tired," Billy said.

Chris grinned. "Okay. Good. Yes, they're all very cool people. They're from an industry where people tend to live their lives every single day. Work hard, party harder, as the saying goes."

"I had a long chat with Steven. He's a great guy and was very inspiring," said Billy.

"He's an amazing guy, and I've been working with him for many years. He understands what I want for my films and does a great job," Chris replied.

Smith came over and took their breakfast order. Chris asked for some toast and eggs, sunny-side up, and Billy ordered scrambled eggs, bacon, and coffee. They were still full from last night's BBQ and drinks.

Tom was very quick in the kitchen, and Smith got their breakfast within a few minutes, along with some orange juice and fresh fruits. Both of them finished their breakfast by the pool and lit their cigarettes.

"We're doing well. So far on track as well," said Chris.

Billy replied, "Yes, sir, we're on time and I guess today it won't be too difficult."

"Yes, today's topics aren't that long, so we can finish them easily by noon and chill in the evening," Chris said with a smile.

"I see you have religiously got your notebook along and kept your recorder ready. So I'll take this as a sign that we can start now. Today's first topic is business planning. A business plan is a formal written document containing the following details. Basic introduction to the business idea, market research and competitor analysis details, company profile, business opportunity, service or product, distribution strategies, risk management, financial flow, targets and the strategies, management and organization chart with detailed job descriptions, processes and operations flow, and an executive summary of the project

"The factors may vary depending on the nature of the business. You might have to add or delete a few points, but mostly, these are the main points that you should include in your business plan. This document serves as a road map that provides direction to the business," said Chris.

"So what is the difference between the brand-identity document and the business-planning document?" Billy asked.

"The brand-identity document is a guideline of how to grow the brand equity by reaching your targeted crowd with the right communication. It's designed to support marketing strategies and decisions for the internal team and brethren. Whereas the business-planning document clearly explains the key details of the project. It's designed to precisely articulate the features of the project," explained Chris.

Chris continued. "I'm glad that you asked this question. You must be wondering what documents need to be prepared, and, fun fact, they all sound the same. Few factors might overlap between documents, but that's a minor glitch. The goal of every document is clearly very different and focused."

"In case of a business-planning document, you should keep it very precise and short. Otherwise, it gets very boring. Imagine reading a long document, and then it loses its purpose and efficiency," finished Chris.

"So what I understand is that this document is a sequel to the setup-and-infrastructure-planning document, which includes the investment required for setting up, launching, and operation expenses as well for a fixed period of time. Is that how it is?" Billy asked.

"In a way, you can say that it's a sequel. The setup-and-infrastructure-planning document is designed to setup the business, whereas the business plan is designed to look forward with time, and the initial version is created based on a hypothesis. It's a plan in totality for the business. It's initial scope of work would involve a forecast of two or three years, and post-launch, the same is reviewed and updated," Chris replied.

"Got it! But I feel it's a good idea to recap the list of documents once we're done with all the topics. I would anyway go back and refer my notes and try to create a table that would help a beginner like me," said Billy.

"Yes, we can keep it as an assignment for you, and then I can check it once you're done. We've spoken about many documents, but the more you detail out before starting off, we'll have a better insight," Chris replied.

"How detailed should be the business-planning document?" asked Billy.

"As I said, don't make it a very long document. Be precise and to the point. That keeps you on track," Chris said.

It was almost 9:00 AM, and Smith came to check if they would like to order for anything. Chris asked for a bloody mary and some water to hydrate himself well. Also, bloody mary was known to be the best cocktail to have if you've had a hard drinking session the previous night. Billy ordered an orange juice and picked up some freshly cut watermelon from the table. Chris continued the conversation.

"One more practice that I suggest to my clients is to add in their business plan the SWOT analysis," said Chris.

Billy said, "SWOT, never heard of that. What does that stand for?"

"SWOT stands for strength, weakness, opportunities, and threats. It's commonly used for the business-analysis process. It ensures that the objectives for the brand are clearly identified, and it also helps understand the speculated success rate of the project," said Chris.

"Oh! That's nice, but how do you do it?" Billy asked.

"It's not as tough as it sounds." Chris smiled. "The whole analysis is divided into internal and external categories. Strengths and weakness fall under the internal bracket, whereas opportunities and threats fall under the external bracket. Let me give you a brief introduction.

"Strengths: the attributes of the project that are considered to be the winners. List all the attributes that you feel would make this project a success. They can be exclusive attributes, why this project should be preferred over competitors. They can be the team. They can also be the distribution chain, good pricing, et cetera.

"Weakness: the attributes of the project that can make it fail. It's very important to identify your weaknesses before itself. That will help you understand the intensity of the weakness, and many times, it might stop you from starting that project. Otherwise, you'll at least be aware of the attributes that you need to be careful about, like too many competitors, no exclusive deliveries, expensive brand, not popular, less margins, high overheads, high investments, et cetera.

"Opportunities: this would include the external factors that you feel would enhance the business or work towards making the business successful. These external factors can be the ease of collaborating with associates, market conditions favoring the project, customers readily accepting the project, et cetera.

"Threats: these external factors would upset the success of the project. These factors need to be studied in detail as they can be the reason for the failure of the project. These factors can be wrong timing, unfavorable market conditions, difficult inventory management cycle, legal issues, change of business regulations, et cetera.

"So that was a brief about all the points, and this much knowledge at this point should be good enough for you to start this process. The more you know your brand and its external environment, the better judgments you can take for the business," concluded Chris.

"I was completely unaware of this SWOT analysis, and I perceive that it's very important for any form of business. Also wanted to check whether we should follow any template for creating the business-planning document?" Billy asked.

Chris replied, "Yes, there are many templates available on the internet that you can use because you have a fair idea about the content. I can also share some the templates my templates."

"That will be really nice, Chris. I'll still do my research," said Billy.

"Good," Chris said and continued. "I would like to make this very clear with you. Our conversations would give you a great insight about how to launch a brand. In some cases, you might have to research more, get your hands dirty, do the ground work, ask around, study the market, speak to professionals, get in touch with experts, et cetera. But you would be in a very comfortable position to do this extensive form of research because you already have a fair idea about the context globally. Once you start working on your brand launch, things would automatically fall in place. By the time I end all my sessions, you'd be close to a pro in the process of launching a new brand." Chris smiled.

***

Chapter 22

Colleagues and Friends

A company culture is the alluring inner force that makes every team member wake up with a smile, with a greedy desire to get to work.

It was 11:00 AM, and Chris decided to take Billy to one of the cafés on South Beach. He quickly went to his room and got into a pair of nice Hawaiian shorts, paired them with a black shooter shirt, and headed towards the Hummer. It was Sunday, and Ron wasn't working. So Chris decided to drive himself and asked Billy to get into the car. Billy kept his crutches in the back seat and hopped into the front seat.

The city looked astounding, more so because it was a Sunday afternoon and the streets were completely empty. They reached South Beach, and the vibe was very happy and chill. They parked the car and walked into an Irish-looking café on the main street. They took a table outside and ordered coffee.

"I just love this street," said Chris.

"It's full of life," Billy remarked. "The feeling is so positive here. People look happy and everyone is in smiles," he continued.

Without wasting any time, Chris began. "Let's get to the second topic of the day, which is brand culture."

"Yeah! This one sounds interesting, and I've been eagerly waiting for it. I always dreamed about working in a place where everyone is having fun, you know, loving what they do, looking forward for the next day at work," said Billy excitedly.

"That's exactly what brand culture does. It defines a group of people practicing a common set of goals, beliefs, practices and values. It's the perception of people about their work, the values they believe, the practices they follow, and how they see themselves being a part of the brand and incorporating its goals. In short, it's the personality of the brand," said Chris.

"Every working individual spends more time at work than at home, leaving aside your sleeping time. So it's imperative for the workplace to be a fun place, a place that everybody looks forward to coming back to every day. It's not the tables and chairs or the décor, but the whole vibe itself that gives them this feeling. To be able to come back with the same energy every single morning," Chris said.

Chris added, "Culture of the brand is equally important for anybody who is part of the brand, irrespective of hierarchy. Every individual is responsible for cascading the brand culture, from the management to the top level and from them to the next level until it reaches the newcomers. It's something that trickles down, so it's very important, especially for the management, to take care of this."

"If you like the vibe of this street, it's just its culture, where you see happy, fun-loving people. This isn't even defined but created over time and passed to the next person without even discussing it. The culture of this street has never changed as it has always attracted the right people, and those who don't like this culture do not come here. It's exactly the same at the workplace. If the culture is strong, you don't really have to talk about it, and it gets transmitted from one batch to another," continued Chris.

"That makes a lot of sense," Billy said.

It was sunny outside and close to lunchtime. Chris called for the steward and ordered two mugs of beer.

"Is there any guideline for creating this right brand culture?" asked Billy.

"I don't believe there is any such guideline. What I believe is that the culture isn't a forced thing, and it has to come naturally to the founders or the management, which then flows toward the employees. Those who love the brand culture slowly mature into being an intrinsic part of it. And those who don't fit in slowly move out of the brand. So there's no perfect brand culture. The best culture may look funny to some, and the worst may even attract some," Chris replied very matter-of-factly.

"Hmm," Billy responded, taking some time to process this, and then asked, "Do you think a relaxed and easy culture works more toward the success of a brand?"

"Yes, absolutely! It works better. Nobody likes to be bullied or forced, whether at work or at home. So when you have more independence at work combined with some fun, then it always works better. As a matter of fact, things have changed a lot now. All the new startups are moving more towards open offices to correlate with an open culture, or have started decorating the workspace with more colors and raw elements to reduce stiffness. Many times, they work and party at the same place, and when work becomes fun, then life looks better, and everybody starts delivering more, leading to brand success," replied Chris.

Chris added, "Remember one thing—satisfaction leads to more productivity, and group satisfaction leads to brand success. That's how important the brand culture role is in creating a successful brand."

"Lastly, do you have any suggestions on how to cascade this culture within the company?" asked Billy.

"Brand culture cascading definitely depends on the existing team, but also a lot on the newcomers. So you have to ensure that you're hiring the right fit for your brand, not just in terms of work profile but also in terms of culture. Every single hiree should fit into the brand culture. You should also check that they match the brand vision, mission, and values. That's the only way you can cascade the culture at ease," Chris replied.

Chris finished his beer and asked for two more mugs for both of them before he continued.

"Let me give you a brief example of one of the best work cultures across the globe. I'm talking about Google. They've topped the list of best companies to work at more than five times, more than 85 percent of their employees are extremely happy to be part of the brand, and they have an exceptional rating on Glassdoor. So this speaks very highly about the amazing culture that persists as the strength of the brand. Google definitely looks a lot into benefits and perks for its employees, but besides that, it has created a very flexible, deliverable-driven culture. The workspaces are always open, very focused on extracurricular activities and great food. They allocate more than $1,000 per individual per year as a party perk, which the team uses every quarter. They provide work-from-home facilities. They're flexible when it comes to paternal and maternal leave. They believe in equal opportunities and are against gender discrimination. They focus on building a strong community, which results in creating a great company culture. Anyone can reach out to anyone with their problems. People are open to meetings and happy to listen. The team believes in the core brand values and ensures that the same is practiced every single day by every single team member. And I don't have to tell you about how successful Google is," said Chris, smiling.

"It's very important for a brand to understand and endorse the fact that 'it's the people who make a brand, and it's only the people who make a brand,'" Chris said. "Let me explain to you about one of my own researches, which I call the *cycle of greatness*."

"That sounds interesting! Is it about how to become great?" asked Billy.

"It's not just about you becoming great but about creating a great brand ecosystem. When I started my journey of entrepreneurship, my thoughts went deep into this subject matter. I don't share this with many people, but I'm happy to share it with you," said Chris.

"I was a firm believer of the fact that it's the people who create successful brands. But at the same time, I always had a question in my mind. All the great people are already working for great brands. And those who are not, always aspire to join the great brands. So, how would a new brand have a great team?"

"This question stayed in my mind for a long time, until I found the missing link. The missing link is you, the founder, the leader. We just need to ensure that we are hiring the right people who can understand the brand vision and love the brand values and culture. Beyond that, it is a great leader who creates a great team. This great team creates a great brand. And with time, the brand evolves and creates more great leaders. And this cycle of greatness grows progressively," Chris said.

They finished the second beer and left. Chris decided to take Billy to one of the best waterside restaurants for lunch.

***

Chapter 23

The Preamble

Create a head for the head, lay down rules for the rulemakers—that's what a constitution does.

They reached the restaurant by the water. It was completely packed, and there was a wait time of fifteen minutes. Billy decided to look around while Chris answered a few emails through his work phone. The restaurant was average looking, with a canopy on top, wooden flooring, and lots of sofas and chairs. But the location made up for the décor, and the food was mouth-watering. It was a forty-three-year-old restaurant, a legacy to the family that owned this restaurant. They were extremely popular for their crabs and prawns. Chris was a seafood lover and knew all the best places to go to. Luckily, they got a table by the water.

The steward was a beautiful-looking young girl named Twanna, who was extremely pleasant and was smiling all the time. She had a glow in her eyes that captivated Billy. There was something about her that he couldn't understand. It moved him from within. Guess "love at first sight" is old school, so let's just say "a good feeling at first sight maybe." Chris ordered for a bottle of white wine with some nuts and cheese.

"Don't you think she's amazing?" Billy whispered .

"Oh really, I didn't see her at all. I was in my own world of thoughts. You like her?" asked Chris.

Billy replied, "I don't even know her. How can I like her? But, yes, there's something about her that draws me towards her."

"So tell her that and ask her out. You have the whole evening. Or you can invite her home for dinner," Chris said.

"Really, Chris, it's that simple? I'm not so good when it comes to women, and on top of that I don't walk now," said Billy sounding a little dejected.

Chris smiled. "This isn't the Billy I know. When did you start making your disability an excuse?"

"Yeah, you're right. Maybe I was just scared to speak to her and was covering up," Billy replied.

Chris smiled. "No, don't be. Just speak to her. Worst case, she is going to say no, which is same as not speaking to her."

"Ok, I'll do it, but not now. Maybe before leaving," said Billy.

They tossed their wine glasses to good health and got back to their conversation. Chris said, "Now coming to the last topic of the day as well as this trip. We did pretty well and managed to complete everything as scheduled. So good job, Billy. All right, moving on, the next topic is company constitution. I'm not referring to the official company constitution."

Billy asked, "What is an official company constitution?"

"Company constitution is a legal document which sets up the rules and regulations governing a company. It defines the relationship between the directors and shareholders. It also includes a set of guidelines to be followed by the shareholders and directors. This is an official requirement while forming a new company," replied Chris.

"Okay, then what is the other version of the company constitution?" Billy asked.

Chris said, "This isn't a document that you'll be guided by any website or brand book. It's purely based on my personal experience as well as many companies that I have associated with. I personally feel that you can name this document whatever you want. This is the boss of the company and can be modified only in the presence and agreement of all the active directors. This document in internal to the top management and especially to the founders."

"So what's the content of this document?" asked Billy.

"This document would be referred in the moment of crisis and conflicts. Many brands start with a noble thought, but with time, things change, and the brand drifts away from its core belief. Any decision that doesn't align with the brand constitution has to be discarded without any conditions. This document remains constant and doesn't change with emotions. Your core beliefs during the time of inception of the brand, including a basic guideline of the culture, would be the main content of this document. It has to be as detailed as possible and should include as many scenarios as possible. So if and whenever, sooner or later, these same scenarios arise, you just need to follow the constitutional directives. There's no set rule to write this document, but it can have everything, especially the pseudo scenarios," Chris said.

Chris added, "Whether it's a brand founded by a single or multiple founders, they're at complete freedom to take any decision in any direction, but not when there's a constitution in place. The constitution would pilot them to take the right decision at any point."

"Does this also include how the founders will work or their internal understanding?" Billy asked.

"Yes, absolutely! It's very important to cover this point in the document. A few random examples would be that the founders won't leave the brand for three years, the founders won't involve in any other business, the founders won't take investors for two years, or the founders will never sell the company. Or there will never be a sale of a product below the company's technical specification (specifications needs to be included here), there will be no change in the pricing policy (policy to be mentioned), et cetera. It's crucial to cover dubious situations in this document as they're the ones that create issues later," said Chris.

Billy said, "Though I haven't completely understood the content, I'm assuming that this document should have an answer to any doubt concerning the directors and we should cover the predicted scenarios for a rainy day more often."

"Yes, Billy, that would be a great start. List down all the yes's and no's, do's, and don'ts for your brand. This document would be the boss of all the bosses and help maintain everything in check, especially with the founders," said Chris.

Chris asked Twanna to take the order for the mains. When she came over, Billy got a little nervous and was unable to decide what he wanted to order. Chris ordered a special prawn dish with baby potatoes.

"Twanna, what a lovely and unique name you have. Why don't you suggest something nice for my friend Billy here?" Chris asked.

"Yes, that would be great," Billy muttered nervously.

She suggested a few dishes, and Billy decided to go for their most popular crab dish.

Billy gathered a lot of courage and finally said, "You have a great smile, Twanna."

Twanna smiled back and replied, "Thank you so much. That was very kind of you."

"Thanks, Chris, for trying to help. Do you think I should ask her out for coffee?" asked Billy.

"Of course, you should!" Chris said with complete confidence.

Chris, being Chris, knew how to get back to the point even when there were a hundred distractions, and so he continued. "Let me tell you something out of context here. If you want, you can put this in the constitution document as well." He smiled.

"Many businesses start with more than one founder. In the beginning, everything looks good, and everybody is positive and deliver their best. But with time, the ideologies and priorities start changing, and this causes rifts between the founders. This is the worst situation you can face, because during this time when you need to focus on making the brand grow, you'll be wasting your time cleaning up differences and massaging egos. As a result, the brand suffers, goes through a turmoil, and the results can be as adverse as failure," warned Chris.

Chris added, "What I'm talking about is a very common trend, and hence, you need to be very clear about having the right business partners. Positive difference of opinion is always healthy, as it gives different perspectives to the brand, but an ego-filled difference of opinion is never healthy. So if your constitution is clear and covers all these points, then you have a better chance of avoiding negative situations."

"Got the point. I would surely spend a lot of time on this document when I form my company so that I can avoid issues in the future," Billy assured.

"I'm glad that we finished all the topics. So with this, you've finished a major part of your learning. I'll need one more day with you, and then you're good to go. In the meantime, I suggest you start thinking about the business you want to start."

"Thank you so much, Chris. I'll work on each and every session we had and make the best use of it. I'm very confident that one day you'll be proud of me, and then I'll come back to your Miami villa again and be your host," said an emotional Billy. Chris could sense the gratitude in his tone.

Chris asked for the bill, but this time, Billy refused to let Chris pay. He said, "I understand that I don't work at the moment, but I also understand and deeply appreciate what you have done for me. I know I cannot repay it, please allow me to take this bill. I insist please," said Billy.

Chris let him pay the bill, and they started moving out. Billy gathered all his courage and went up to Twanna. "Hey, Twanna! You're extremely beautiful, and there's something about you that connected with me the first time I saw you. I thought I shouldn't leave this place without telling you this. I'm from Chicago, and I'm here till tomorrow evening. If at all you're free and ok to catch up for a coffee this evening or tomorrow first half, I would be extremely happy." Billy gave his phone number to her and left for the car.

They reached the villa by 4:00 PM. Chris was glad that he'd completed the scheduled sessions before time. He went to his room to catch up on his work while Billy chilled by the pool. Chris had an early-morning flight. He had booked the return tickets for Billy and Smith in the evening so that they could enjoy one whole day without any work in Miami.

In the evening, Chris went out to meet some of his friends. Billy spent time talking to his family, Sean, and then hanging out with Smith and Tom by the pool. It was a trip to be cherished and remembered forever.

Twanna texted Billy in the evening, and they chatted for a long time. She wasn't free in the evening, so Billy missed the opportunity to meet her, but she never left his mind. He knew he would see her again very soon.

***

Chapter 24

One Collaborates with One and Equals Eleven

You have a little, someone else has a little. Put it together, you get a whole. This is the secret to success. Collaborate.

Billy woke up early Tuesday morning with one of the best hangovers of his life. The most incredible trip. He was sad it was over, but he was also looking forward to meeting his family. Over breakfast, they all connected again like they used to, and he was narrating his trip excitedly, just like how a child would when speaking about his favorite game. He was so ecstatic while sharing his experience that they could see the happiness in his eyes. His family was deeply moved by Chris and how well he had taken care of Billy. They told Billy how fortunate he was to have such a kindhearted mentor. Asha was extremely fascinated by Chris and never expected that he would go out of his way and help Billy while sharing his proficiency. They all wished Billy a great future, and they all had faith that he would be a very prosperous entrepreneur.

Billy spent the rest of the day organizing himself at home, putting all his travel clothes to wash while recovering from an eventful trip. He called his friends and asked if they could all catch up the next day. He had some plans for his friends and decided to meet and have a conversation with them. This was important for him and even for them.

The Grahams had early dinner, and they discussed Billy's business ideas, the fact that he wanted to share this idea with his friends and see if they would be interested to be part of it. His family was always supportive of whatever he wanted to do but advised him to be very careful in choosing the right partners for his business. They had only one main worry. Billy was a reformed person now and should not get back to his old habits again. Deep down, they had the confidence that he was a changed and matured boy now and would never let them down again. They also believed that he had the charisma to bring his friends to the right path.

Next morning, Billy and his friends decided to meet at Whalon Lake at 10:00 AM. Over the last few months, Billy has been highly inspired by Chris and his family. There were lessons all around him—he just had to open his mind and accept them. A few of the biggest lessons he learned from all were to be calm, keep an open mind, be close to nature, and always be eager to be a better version of himself. Inspired by Chris and his dad, he decided to organize all his meetings in an open environment.

Sean picked up Billy on his way. They all reached the lake on time and found a captivating corner on the bank of the lake. They got some food and drinks from the supermarket. They were five of them from the gang—Sean, Phil (a super-tech-friendly boy), Dylan (who was a charmer and extremely pleasant), Fia (who was a social media superhero and also ran a very popular blog), and Billy. They had no clue why Billy wanted to meet them, and it was more surprising to them that they weren't meeting in any of their regular hangout places. They all knew that it had to be something special and were eagerly waiting to hear from Billy.

"So what's the deal, Billy? Why did you call us here?" asked Phil.

"We have a big circle of friends, but I decided to specifically call the four of you and share some of my thoughts that have been constantly going on at the back of my mind. Maybe you can connect to whatever I'll be sharing with you today," Billy said.

Billy continued, "Before I come to the point, let me share with you some of my personal feelings. I understand that we had a lot of fun. We've done good and bad, but when I saw death so close, I realized the true meaning of this beautiful thing called *life*. We never really tried to understand that life has a deeper meaning. We believed in having fun, and we lived for the moment. We never really respected our loved ones, and we did what we always wanted to do. It's absolutely right to love yourself, but not at the cost of being acutely selfish. We just cared for our happiness and not for anyone around us, not even for our family.

"I'm so sorry that I'm sounding like someone who hates you guys, but that's not true. I really care, which is why I'm here sitting and talking to you. I always wanted to share my realization. After my second chance at life, I realized that so far I have lived a life of loss and regret. Loss of my limb and regrets from my past. But in this loss and regret I have seen gains and opportunities, like never before. Sorry, I maybe sounding like your folks, but I want the best for you. I'm sharing my feelings, and I pray that none of you experience what I've gone through. So I want you guys to please take five minutes and give an honest thought to whatever I have said just now."

They all took time and reached deep within themselves and thought about what Billy said just now. "I guess you're partially wrong, Billy. We do what we like, and that's how it's supposed to be, isn't it?" asked Fia.

"There's a big difference between living *for* the moment and living *in* the moment. We lived for the moment, which isn't right at all. That's against humanity. I also understand that we shouldn't hook on to the past and worry about the future, but we should live in the moment. I also said the same thing, that we're supposed to love ourselves, but not at the cost of others' happiness. There are many times when we've disappointed many people, including our families. I realized this when I was in the hospital. They were ready to give up their lives for mine. Now ask yourself this: Did we ever think like that?" Billy asked.

"After my accident, I didn't want to meet any of you. I felt that I was a vegetable, a dead person, and a handicap for life. I also felt it was because of my friends and our deeds. I was unable to get over my loss and regrets. But very soon, I saw the reality of life. Whatever happened to me was purely because of my own deeds, and nobody else had anything to do with it. That's when I came back to you guys and even spoke to Sean about it. My purpose was to forget the past and take out all the negativity from my mind, especially against my friends. And it worked. I felt good, I felt lighter, and now I'm here sitting and talking to all of you from the bottom of my heart," said Billy.

Billy added, "Yes, it's great to have fun and enjoy life, but it's also our responsibility to take care of the rights and the wrongs. It's a very thin line and we should be careful not to cross it. You don't have to convince anybody else. Just convince yourself that you're not doing anything wrong. Then everything's cool."

"I completely understand what you're saying, Billy," said Sean. "I also had similar feelings like yours after the accident. I was deep in guilt. This fight happened because of me, and you almost lost your life. It was killing me every single day until you called me, met me, and gave me the confidence that you want to forget about whatever happened. My heart was filled with respect for you, and I wished that day that you become a very successful person. I also realized that there's no space for shortcuts in life. What happened to you could have happened to me or any of us. You're strong, and you came back with full power, but some might give up," added Sean.

"I also almost gave up. I felt like I was a living burden to my family until I went to We Care and met those lovely kids. Some of them were even in a worse state than me, but they still had smiles and were happy about life. That was the moment of realization, and here I am today, standing strong and making a statement in my life. Life has been really good after that. I've had the best of my experiences, and I'm sure this is just the beginning," said Billy.

"I wanted to tell you guys that I have a mentor who's very popular in the advertising industry. He's an amazing personality and has been mentoring me for quite some time. I just got back from Miami day before, where I had an exclusive mentorship weekend in his private villa. I have a dream, and he's been helping me prepare for my dream," Billy said.

"What's your dream, Billy?" asked Dylan.

"Well, I want to own and run a place like We Care, where we help the underprivileged, poor, and needy. This organization will completely take care of them and help them fight depression, stay healthy, and be good people and independent human beings. But for that, you need money, which I don't have. So in an effort to reach there, I want to start my business first, and then when I have enough money, I can start my own We Care," Billy said. "I want to make this life meaningful and I'm here talking to all of you to ask if you guys would like to join me in this journey."

All four of them were taken aback. They weren't sure how to react to Billy's question. They never saw this coming their way. They were all having fun and enjoying life, and suddenly, this heavy sense of responsibility hit them like a cold blast of air.

"But how can we be a part of this journey? I'm unable to understand your proposition completely," a perplexed Phil said.

"Yes, even I fail to understand what you want us to do," Fia joined in, looking worried.

"I want all of us get together, form a company, and start our business. We all are twenty-one, and there are many millionaires and few billionaires less than our age. So if we put our acts together and be focused and work dedicatedly towards our goal, we can do it as well," said Billy, making an impressive effort to inspire his friends.

"But how, Billy? We don't have any knowledge, we don't have any experience, and why do you think we can do it? Honestly, I have never even thought about anything like this, forget about *doing* it," said Phil with lot of honesty.

"How is never the problem. Whether you have, the will is more important. If you decide to do it, then we'll figure out a way together," said Billy.

They were all attracted by Billy's positivity and optimism and were drawn towards the idea of making their life meaningful. They also loved the fact that they could be successful entrepreneurs. They were getting excited about it but also scared at the same time. They all knew that this was the moment to make an important decision in their life, and none of them expected it to come this way, with absolutely no warning at all. But whatever it was, they had a good feeling about it.

"Okay, assuming we all agree, then what's next?" demanded Fia still confused.

"I'm almost completing my sessions with Chris. Once that's done, then I was planning to work on the business plan. You guys don't have to be scared about the business model and other technical details. I can do a crash course for you guys, and then we can start working together. We all need to think about a good business idea and start working on it. Rest will automatically fall into place," Billy assured them.

"I'm sure it's not as simple as it sounds now," said Sean.

"It's not. We really have to work hard. Let me tell you a few things. You'll need to give up on everything else and focus on the business. You'll need to bring in your part of the investment. You should say yes only when you're committed to the final goal of doing something like We Care. If it's about making personal money, then you shouldn't be a part of this project. I would like to work with a team that believes in the final goal and works with dedication toward it. Even if later you want to do something of your own, that's fair. So I want you guys to sleep on it, and we can meet again and take a call. You can discuss the same with your families as well," Billy said. "This decision is going to change your life, from being boys and girls to men and women, from being kids to CEOs and CFOs. It's not going to happen overnight. It's days of toil and nights of burning the midnight oil, but in the end, it's all worth it. You need to feel this way for us to discuss more."

They all sat there in silence, taking it all in. The funnyman Sean broke the silence with a joke about how Phil would look in a red suit and yellow shirt. The mood lightened up, and everybody spoke about Billy's sessions with Chris. There was a positive excitement. They had a few more questions, which Billy answered honestly. They all headed back home and thanked Billy for considering them to be a part of his dream journey. They decided to meet at the same time, same place, after two days.

Thursday, 10:00 PM, Billy was in his bed falling asleep. He couldn't help but wonder about the following day. Was he close to achieving his dreams? Were his friends going to be in? Had he made the right choice by speaking to them so soon? Hundreds of thoughts raced his mind. He let out a deep, exhausted breath and smiled. A nice wide smile. This Billy wasn't going to worry. Version 2.0 only got the best of him. He knew deep down that he was working toward his goals, to be successful, to make the world a better place. And this he would do. He was a man with a plan. His thoughts drifting away, he was soon fast asleep.

Friday morning, 10:00 AM, they all met at the same place. They looked happy and excited for the meeting.

"Good morning, guys!" Billy said. "What's happening?"

"Hey, Billy! Doing good. What's up with you?" Fia replied, looking calm, unlike their last meeting.

"All good and excited to hear from you guys," replied Billy.

"We all thought about what we discussed on Wednesday. We discussed it amongst ourselves and also with our parents. Things looks positive. In fact, our parents were astoundingly pleased to hear about the whole idea. There are few points that we need to discuss and to be confident about this project, which I guess will happen over time," Sean replied.

"So good to hear that, and I'm looking forward to doing this together with you guys. I'm sure we will make it big," said Billy. "Until now, we've done good and bad in our lives. It was due to personal stress, family stress, our surroundings, or an aimless desire to have fun. But that was our past, and let's leave it there. Now we've decided to break all barriers and bring goodness to ourselves, our families, and the people around us. I can't tell you how excited I am to hear your positive reply. This is just the beginning, and I can see the sun rising."

"So, Billy, what's next?" Dylan asked with excitement. He was the wise and calm one in the gang of friends. Dylan had already been sold by this idea the first time he'd heard it, but he hadn't expressed himself because he hadn't wanted to influence the crowd in anyway. He wanted everyone to think for themselves.

"Let me structure this whole thing so that we all are on the same page. Why don't we all sit down and be comfortable. This is going to take a long time," replied Billy.

They sat down by the lake. Sean had brought a lot of stuff to eat and drink. Billy asked for a Cola and started the conversation, "This discussion is about starting a business. So I hope all of us understand that for the first time in our lives, we're getting into some real serious matters. It's not just about our money and efforts but also our time and confidence. So we don't have any other option but to be focused and dedicated. Can I hear a yes from all of you?" asked Billy beaming with confidence.

Every single person agreed with him and said that they understood the call of commitment and they all were ready to be focused and driven.

"Now that we all understand the intensity of the commitment, we have to be very careful about our basic behavior. If we want to build a great company, then we need to display and practice highest levels of ethical behavior. These are the basics of starting a company together. Are we in agreement to this?" Billy asked. They all agreed happily.

Billy continued. "It's always a task to have a group of people to work as partners and form a company. The biggest brands have gone through partnership breaks, which end up being very nasty and disturbing. The top advice before forming a company is to partner only with like-minded people who share the same values and passion. We all have been friends for many years, but now we're going to work on a serious business plan, and differences will crop up with time. Differences are a part of partnerships, but how well you handle differences is important. In the beginning, everything seems nice and rosy, but with time, we change, so do our priorities, and that's when differences arise. We have a much bigger goal to achieve, which has a greater meaning. Only if all of us are focused on the bigger goal and don't bring our egos to work, we can be successful," said Billy. This would surely have been a proud moment for Chris if he had heard it.

"Many companies split or shut down due to partnership problems. Why does this happen?" asked Dylan.

"I had asked the same question to Chris. Let me explain what he said. First of all, it's important to understand why companies are started in partnerships. Do you have any idea why it happens?" asked Billy.

"People decide to work or launch a new project together, and hence, they form partnership companies, no?" questioned Phil.

"Ok, that's one of the ways. Most people get together to form a company either if they don't have enough funds to start off with or people with different strengths get together to form a company. That helps the company have multiple talents working on different verticals. This makes the company extremely strong. In our case we have a mix of both the reasons—less capitals and also our strengths," said Billy. "Now coming to the main point—why partnerships split. If the partners are careful about a few factors, then a partnership can never break. There are many factors that they need to be careful about, but the top four that come to my mind are transparency, ethics, ego and clear division of responsibilities.

"Transparency. There should be transparency maintained between all the partners to avoid any misunderstandings. Anything that comes across cloudy to any of the partners becomes a trigger to start losing trust. Also, all critical decisions at a company level should be discussed with all partners. Hence, regular meetings help avoid miscommunication.

"Ethical. There's no excuse for unethical behavior, especially in a partnership-based company. Sometimes, we get so blinded by the momentary benefits that we lose focus on the bigger goal. This usually leads to splitting of partnerships as this isn't forgivable professionally. And no matter how much we try to hide, any form of unethical behavior would eventually be visible to the other partners within time.

"Ego. Partnership is like a marriage, which demands understanding, professional respect, and small compromises. We should always leave our egos at home. Differences of opinion are always healthy for a company to reach a wider range of ideas and then pick the best among them. But when egos come into play, then the results can never be fair. If the partners are focused on the bigger goal, then surely they will manage to keep all egos out of their conversations.

"Work division. This is a very important factor for crumbling of partnerships. When partners don't involve themselves equally, then it raises questions in the mind of the partner who is devoting more time to the company. That's why all partners need to focus equally in building the company. Short-term differences are fine, but long-term differences should always be spoken about before starting the company so that shares and salaries are equated accordingly. If this exercise is done before the situation soars up, then it can be controlled as everybody is fairly aware of the same.

"Partnership is as easy as it is hard. If we maintain and follow these rules, then there's a very less likelihood of any partnership collapsing," said Billy.

"Let's all work on a few smaller assignments, like naming the company, deciding on the business, doing some research on the different considered business, and probably a small event for the underprivileged. If we're able to work together as a team on these pilot projects, then let's go ahead and form the company and start working on our business. Else, if we feel one of us should not be a part of this, then let's be honest and fair and not have any hard feelings. It's for the better future of the company. We'll always be friends," said Billy.

"Also, today, I'm doing the initial talking, but once we're in place, then we all would be equal partners, and we'll focus on our own responsibilities and work as a team. We'll contribute to our best capacities so that the company benefits the most. We all have diverse talents, and if we use our individual talents in a disciplined manner, then success is ours," added Billy confidently.

Dylan said, "Billy, what you said makes complete sense. I personally agree with this. No hard feelings at all. We will try and see if it works out between us and then let's all take a collective decision. Prevention is always better than cure. Also, I personally feel that we'll be a good team and do great together."

"I would like to add that it's very important to do the right business in terms of opportunity as well as our passion. So let's not compromise at all in deciding the right business, even if it takes time," Billy said.

They all took a quick smoke break and picked up some snacks and drinks. Although Billy was very straight, everybody appreciated his openness for the better health of their relationships. They had a sense of acceptance that Billy was in a better position to speak at this moment because he had been doing a lot of research and actively involved in mentorship sessions, so he brought more knowledge to the table at this point of time.

After the break, they all sat together and brainstormed over the company's name. They did that for more than two hours, which was a great team exercise and created a sense of belonging as they started working on building their dream collectively.

***

Chapter 25

The Magic Mantras

Billions of people in our planet, only a few wind up in your company. And that's what we call destiny. It's you who can make them belong to the company, only when you believe that it's they who will build the company.

Billy went to Chris's penthouse the following Saturday at 10:00 AM. Chris had finished his Saturday morning run and was enjoying his avocado smoothie by the pool. Smith was extremely happy to see Billy, so was Chris.

Chris smiled. "How have you been, Billy? Feels like we haven't met in ages."

"So true, and it hasn't even been two weeks," Billy replied. He also ordered a Smith special avocado smoothie.

"What's going on, Billy? Hope your family was happy to see you back," said Chris.

"They were definitely happy to see me, but they were happier to know the details of the trip. They really appreciate your kindness and asked me to give their regards to you," Billy said humbly.

"Don't worry about that, Billy. I'm very happy to do the best I can for you. Please convey my regards to them," replied Chris.

"Last week, I met four of my friends. I shared the idea of forming a company and starting a business together. They are very excited about it, and we're now working on smaller assignments to understand our compatibility as partners. Only if we feel that we can be a great team will we take this forward. I also spent a lot of time working on my notes and audiotapes from our sessions. So I have been working a lot and been having a great time," Billy said.

Chris smiled. "Oh that's wonderful. I'm glad you started working on your dream. I hope you're being very careful in choosing the right partners as five people is a big number to form a company," he advised.

"Yes, I have also been very open in expressing this to them. If we feel that any of us can't be a part of a team, then that person is out. They understood and acknowledged it," Billy replied.

"Do you want some beer, Billy?" asked Chris.

"I actually don't mind. I didn't go out at all the past two weeks," Billy replied.

They picked up their beer and sat on the sofa by the bar. It was a nice, sunny morning, and both the gentlemen got to business straight away. Billy wasn't sure about the agenda for the day.

"We've already completed all the factors that you need to know before launching a brand. You have a good understanding about it now and you can think about working on launching your brand. However before doing that, there are few points which you should keep in mind that will help you take better decisions to run a successful company," said Chris.

"Are these factors related to the brand launch?" asked Billy.

"Not directly, but important points to know before starting your company for sure. It's more important to understand their importance rather than what they do," Chris replied.

"So, the factors that we will discuss today are-the idea, the people, business model, timing, the product, patience, and simplicity and transparency.

"All these points are very important for the success of the brand, and we'll briefly discuss them. We'll also discuss the hierarchy of importance of these points. Once you're aware and careful about how these factors influence your business, it will put you in a much better position to start your business."

"I understand what you mean. This sounds interesting," said Billy.

"More than 130,000 startups get launched on a daily basis across the globe, out of which less than 10 percent succeed. There are many factors that build the success story of a brand, but the ones I just mentioned are on top of the list. A business or a brand always starts from an idea. So the idea becomes the root of it. A strong business idea is one of the most important factors for the its success. However, if the idea isn't executed well, then a great idea gets wasted," said Chris.

"I understand that the best idea has to be well executed to be successful," Billy repeated.

"Absolutely! It's very important to have a great idea and that's why this is in my list of important factors to be considered for a successful business. Don't even think about starting your business unless it's a great idea. First, you should be convinced that it's a good idea and research casually by talking to your friends and family about the idea. Many times, we get blinded and biased by our own ideas and see only the best things from it. Never bring your ego and emotions while deciding a business idea, because later, that might cost a lot. Be very open to feedback, analyze it from every possible direction. Remember that you're not going to buy your products. It's the people who will buy your products. When you talk to a few people about the idea, you'll realize where it stands," said Chris.

Chris continued. "The idea is eventually going to turn into a product or a service, which would eventually be the core of the business. It's true that the trust, faith, hope, investments and plans all fall into place because of a great idea. That's why we say a business starts with a great idea."

"How do we gauge a good idea?" asked Billy.

Chris said, "Well, there are no defined parameters, but I can give you some direction, which might help you decide if it's a good idea. First of all, you need to check if the idea is solving a problem or making life easier for the world and if people would love to adapt to it. If yes, then it's a no-brainer that it's a great idea. So an exclusive idea that can make a difference to the existing current ecosystem is always a great idea."

"You have to consider whether the idea is different and also difficult to implement. If it's a new but easily replicable idea and can't be patented, then you have to give it a second thought. Sometimes a good idea gets launched and then the giants pick the same idea and make it bigger. So it's always better that the idea is difficult to be replicated. Even if it does get replicated, it may take some time, and by then you'd get the first-move advantage," said Chris.

"Some other factors that can make an idea great are if it has a great demand (mask and sanitizers during COVID-19). It can be an existing idea but with a great value add (Facebook over Myspace). It can be a supplier to a much bigger idea (delivery support to all online selling platforms). It can be an aggregator of a very successful category (Expedia) and more. But again, you need to remember that, an idea would become great only when it's executed well," said Chris, smiling.

Like always, Billy was impressed and enlightened. Every minute spent with Chris, he felt that he was learning a lot, but he also got the feeling that he had a lot more to learn. Chris lit his cigarette and asked for one more beer. So did Billy. The sun was getting stronger; the day was passing soon, but the weather stayed beautiful.

Chris got back to the conversation, "The next point is one of the most important factors for me personally—the people. Have you ever thought why great brands have great people?"

"If the brand is good and big, then many people want to join them, and they pick only the best," Billy replied.

"That's partially true, but the fact is that it's actually the people who made the brand great. It has always been like this; all great brands are created by great people. Many fail to understand this very simple success secret. No big activity can be done alone; you need a great team to do that. No war was won alone by an emperor, but by his great army. You definitely need great leaders to show the vision and then make them live the vision and win the battle for you," said Chris.

"Then you really need to be lucky to have great people in your company. That may not be possible every time. What do we do then?" Billy asked.

"That's not true. It's a *cycle of greatness*. Great leaders in the company create great people, and great people together create a great brand. So you should know how to make people great. They may not be as good when they join you, but with time, they'll adapt themselves and become great. Does that make sense?"

"Yes, I got the point that we need to be good leaders to prepare good people. Would love to hear how you do that?" asked Billy.

Chris said, "The most important factor is to establish the right culture. The right culture will keep the team positive and happy, eventually resulting to great productivity. A great culture will treat everybody with equality and honesty. It will build the team's trust and allow them to give their best towards every decision of the management. Also, a great culture will help the weaker get better and fit into the team. You need to create opportunities for them to grow. They should be able to visualize their growth along with the brand's growth. That's when you get the best from them."

He continued. "It cannot be a parasitic relationship, which many old school organizations still practice. There's always give and take. Some decision may be hard for the management as well, but they still take them only to put the wellbeing of the team first."

"They need to have a strong sense of belonging to the brand, considering the brand as their own. Many leaders know the importance of this statement but never work towards achieving it. You have to value and profoundly feel that it's the people who make the brand, and that's when you'll be able to give them a feeling of belongingness. And once you inculcate this feeling, then the battle is won," said Chris.

"You need to create a platform where they learn every single day. It's very important that they grow as better professionals every day. There should be a take home for them every single day. They need to grow on their technical skills, on their management skills, and the leaders have to provide them this opportunity to grow," Chris said.

Chris concluded. "Don't worry about hiring great people. If you have the ability you will create great people. So you should align yourself and your partners to follow this."

"We've already had a detailed discussion about the next point, which is the business model. We've already had a conversation on how to make a good business model. I have included this point here again because this is an important factor for the success of the company. You have to follow all the steps we discussed and ensure that you have a great business model. Also you need to be careful about not making a perfect business model before the launch. Many people spend a lot of time in making a perfect business model, and the brand launch gets delayed. The business model can be reiterated once you start and slowly it will strike a balance. I would specifically like to emphasize on one point from the business model which is cash flow. You have to have a great insight into the cash flow, as this is the deciding factor for the success of the brand," said Chris.

"Well noted," said Billy.

"How about a few appetizers, Billy?" asked Smith.

"Perfect timing, thank you so much, Smith. I'm hungry and would love to have some," Billy replied.

"Well, that's the next topic," said Chris.

Billy was muddled and didn't understand the context of appetizers with the next topic. "Sorry, I didn't understand," he said.

Chris smiled. "The next topic is about timing."

"Oh yeah, I got it now. I got confused back there," said Billy, smiling back.

"That's ok. We were deep in our conversation, and suddenly, I correlated an appetizer with the next topic. But to my relief, Smith asked for the appetizers at the most appropriate time. If he had asked you for appetizers when you came, you would've said no, since you already had your breakfast before coming here. And if he asks you again sometime later before lunch, you would say no since you were going for lunch or probably you already had some appetizers now. The same way, every business has the right time to be launched. If it's launched before time, then there are chances that it will fail, and if it's delayed then someone would have already taken the market share, just like your appetizer," said Chris with a laugh.

"Wow, that was perfect. Was that planned, Chris?" Billy asked.

"No way. Do you think I'll make a plan with Smith on the timing for appetizers?"

"I guess not," replied Billy in a goofy manner.

"Maybe it's a sign that you're learning well. Coming back to our point, timing is again one of the most important factors for the success of any business. Facebook was great, but its timing with the exponential growth of smart phones revolutionized the brand," Chris said.

Smith got them some appetizers. They got one more round of beer and sat on the bar stool. Billy had never seen a passionate teacher like Chris. This revealed why he was such a successful person.

Chris moved on. "The next topic is about the product. Every brand strives to develop a product or a service, and for the ease of conversation, I'm considering both a product. The product is the core of your brand and there's absolutely no way you can make it a lower priority. Many brands get so focused on their revenues and profits that the product life cycle doesn't matter to them. In a successful brand, every single team member is working towards creating a great product. They understand the value and work relentlessly toward perfecting the product."

"This would always be kept in mind all the time, Chris. I'll ensure that the product always gets priority. A failed product is a failed brand in the long run," said Billy in complete agreement with Chris.

"Also, Billy, you need to be very careful about another important factor. When a brand is getting launched, everybody works toward creating a great product. The best possible product is created and then launched successfully. But you need to understand that a product needs constant improvements and upgradations. You need to innovate constantly. If you take the example of any successful brand, like Apple, Microsoft, Facebook, you'll see a common trend— they have always kept their product history interesting and they're growing all the time. There has to be constant research and development dedicated to product enhancements," added Chris. "So it's not just at the beginning, but throughout the life of the brand. So now you can say that the product is one of the most important factors for the success of the brand."

Billy retorted, laughing, "From my lessons, almost everything is an important factor for the brand."

Chris smiled and let Billy enjoy his little joke. And that's why brand building is as tough as climbing a mountain.

It was almost lunchtime, but Chris decided to continue with the conversation as they had only two topics left. He ordered for lunch to be served within half an hour and a refill of their beer. He walked up to the railing and enjoyed his cigarette alone, then came back to the sofa and found Billy already seated there.

"The next topic is 'patience' and how is that supposed to help a brand?" asked Billy impatiently, adding to the irony of the situation.

Chris laughed and answered, "Patience has nothing to do with brand building. But it's an important factor that a successful brand exhibits. Today's world is dynamic, and everybody expects instant gratification. Many companies want to become a brand as soon as they get launched which is mostly not possible. A brand is built over time, and there are multiple factors that makes a brand, a brand. If you don't have the right level of patience and don't understand the art of building a brand, you might give up midway. And that's why patience is essential in the process of building a successful brand," said Chris.

"Like they say, patience is a virtue. Got it. I never thought that way. But why would someone give up halfway?" questioned Billy.

"To build a brand, you need to do a lot of planning, especially time management. The market is always volatile and in momentum. This means there would be lots of changes in your brand strategies to adapt to the ever changing market. So if you're not agile and haven't planned your growth well, you'll run out of cash and patience and be left with no other option but to give up. Also in today's world, whether it's an online purchase, a food order, or anything else you want to buy, it can be ordered in a matter of seconds and received at your doorstep. When we're living in a world of luxury and instant results, nobody has the patience. People have forgotten to wait. So impatience and the lack of instant gratification make people quit. They feel they are unable to make an impact, or they are unable to build the brand, not understanding that it takes time to create a brand," Chris replied. "Many brands drift away from their values with time due to the urgency of making quick profits. In this process, the product, which is the core of the brand, suffers, leading to brand-identity dilution. So you need to be very clear, focused, and work patiently to build the right brand."

"Now, we finally come to the last point—simplicity and transparency. These two attributes are to be used internally and externally. As a brand, you'll have your own values, but these two should definitely appear in the top of that list," said Chris.

"Can you please explain the impact of both these attributes to the internal team as well as to the external market?" asked Billy, trying his best to understand while making notes.

"Leonardo da Vinci said, 'Simplicity is the ultimate sophistication', simplicity is an extremely important factor for building a successful brand. Most successful brands work towards making life simple for their customers. But one must understand that achieving this is the toughest job. Simplicity isn't easy to achieve. Simplicity is about clarity. Clarity in your thoughts, clarity in your actions, clarity in what you promise to your client, clarity in what your clients expect from your brand. If there's something about your brand that's difficult to understand for the internal team, then there's no way your customers will understand it. The ideologies and the guidelines of the brand should always be simplified. For example, look at the products of Apple. They're highly simplified in terms of design and usability. At the same time, they know how to keep it exclusive and classy," said Chris.

Chris continued, "Transparency is about truth, and it's about people believing in your brand. You cannot lie and make a brand. Any lie is going to come out to your customers or your internal team at some point of time. A brand is a promise, and transparency is the only way to make your customers believe in your promise. Transparency has to be practiced internally, and then it resonates to your customers automatically. Internally, it defines consistency in what you do every day and that's what builds the brand.

"To put it straight—always keep things easy, simple, and transparent to build a great brand," concluded Chris.

"Thank you again, Chris. Every time I meet you, I feel so enlightened. There's a strong positive vibe resonating within me, urging me to see all this happening in the real world. Also one thing that I'll take with me forever is that no matter how much I know, there's always a lot more to learn and I'll never let this drive lose momentum. I'll always find avenues to gather more knowledge and be a better human every single day," said Billy, smiling shyly.

"Always keep your hunger for knowledge alive. That's the only way one can be successful and a better human being. I'm glad you have that realization. There's always so much knowledge around us. We just need to create the urge to gather it," Chris said. "So, let me summarize, we've listed six points, and if you have to rank them in order of importance, how would you?" asked Chris.

"That's a difficult one. Everything looks important to me, but since you're asking, here goes my sequence. Firstly, the idea, secondly the product followed by the business model, then the people, fifthly simplicity and transparency, then timing, and lastly patience. "Am I close? Is this right?" Billy asked impatiently, hoping he was right.

"You were right about all the factors being equally important, but research has something else to say. This is how the ranking is: timing, people, idea, business model, the product, simplicity and transparency, and patience. What do you have to say about that?" asked Chris, teasing Billy.

"It's so difficult to believe that timing tops the list. But I'm sure it has its own reasons, so I won't argue," said Billy.

"Yes, a brand launched too early or too late has a higher probability of failure. Right timing can make the journey very easy for a brand to reach success. All these factors are important, but I gave you this order so you understand it better and can reason it out yourself. Once you launch your brand, you'll automatically know why this order is as such." Chris smiled and continued. "So don't give less importance to the last ones, okay? All right then, we're done, Billy! You're good to start your brand now," said Chris confidently.

"You mean I'm done with all lessons or I'm done only for today?" Billy asked.

"Yes, you're done for good. I have taught you everything you need to learn to create a brand. From here, you're on your own and you have to keep gathering knowledge by yourself to get better," said Chris.

"Oh! This was so sudden," Billy said sadly.

"You can always schedule a meeting with me, if you feel like catching up. I would love to hear from you and see how your company is doing," said Chris politely.

"Let me take this opportunity to thank you from the bottom of my heart. You're the kindest person I have ever come across. I understand and appreciate each and every moment you invested in me. In fact, you went out of your way many times to ensure that I got the best in the best possible way. Thank you again, Chris, and I'm forever grateful to you. I'll do my best to create a great brand and make you proud. Thank you, thank you!" exclaimed Billy with mixed emotions.

They had lunch together, silently. Billy was sad to realize that he wouldn't be meeting Chris as he did in the past, but at the same time, he hoped that this beautiful relationship would last forever.

***

Chapter 26

United for a Cause

Life is the best gift for humanity. Make this eternal gift meaningful by adding a cause to it.

Monday morning, 10:00 AM, Billy and his friends met at a café near Billy's house. They all went together to We Care for a while, played with the kids, and distributed fruits and chocolates they'd brought for them. Although they stayed there for a short while, they felt what Billy and Sean felt. Billy wanted them to experience and understand the feeling of giving and caring and the positivity from every single kid at We Care. From there, they all went to a park around the neighborhood. Billy always believed in having important discussions in an open environment, amidst nature. He believed that this helped keep one's mind peaceful and open.

They picked a private nook surrounded by trees. They had a long and a very important day ahead. They were finalizing the name of the company as well as discussing various business ideas. Everybody had made a list of names for their company and shared their lists, with the meaning and the concept behind the names. Many names were really good, with great meanings. They wanted the company's name to be meaningful and timeless. The name had nothing to do with the brand name as that was a different exercise itself after they'd decide on their business idea. The brainstorming activity went beyond two hours, and they were fully engrossed in selecting the company name. They weren't used to such long sessions and were taking quick breaks in between the conversation. That was also helping them keep their mind fresh. Finally, after everybody put their thoughts on the table, they decided to go with the name suggested by Dylan—United for a Cause Pvt. Ltd. They all unanimously agreed and loved the name. They liked its simplicity, it was why they came together and it will remind them of their goals all the time. Also this name was timeless and classy. A job well done and Billy was happy about the fact that there was no ego tussle in deciding the name. The moment they named their company, they felt a stronger bond between themselves. That was the power of an identity.

They grabbed lunch at the food truck stationed at the end of the park. There was a small speaker in the food truck which was playing some Neil Diamond classics, setting the perfect mood. There were benches around the truck, and they sat in one of the tables. They had burgers and hot dogs with some sodas and colas to keep it light and quick.

They got back to the same place after lunch and continued their conversation. Billy decided to tell them about what he learnt from Chris. So he started with how he'd met Chris and how the mentoring had begun. Then slowly, he moved to the important topics and explained every single topic briefly. He started with the purpose of the brand and its importance, and then he moved to all the crucial factors that needed to be implemented before launching a brand and then finally the essentials to be considered for a successful business.

The conversation went on for five long hours, and all his friends were highly impressed with Billy's knowledge. Billy was extremely happy that he could share his knowledge with his partners and going forward they will be able to correlate their discussions. They all thanked Billy for sharing his knowledge and putting the effort in educating them. They also appreciated the fact that this was completely Billy's initiative and he could have always kept a bigger share for himself in the company and everybody would have happily agreed. But Billy refused to do so; he wasn't looking at personal benefits here. They were all working for a bigger cause, and when the bigger cause was achieved, these things wouldn't matter to them. He had set up a great example of being transparent and selfless in creating the company, and this would surely take them a long way and ensure that his partners also start thinking the same way. Billy always believed in doing and setting an example rather than telling people what and how to do things.

After five long hours of technical discussions, United for a Cause decided to go to a bar and grab some beer. They were all happy to be together and were doing a lot of constructive work, with a common goal in place. They went to Harry's and enjoyed their well-deserved evening.

For the next few days and weeks, United for a Cause kept meeting every day. They had discussions about different prospective businesses, executed one small event, and came up with numerous thoughts and ideas for the company. When five people worked dedicatedly towards one goal every day, they were bound to achieve results.

They finished all the official formalities for the formation of a company. They finalized on three tentative business ideas and decided to do a small market research and then closed on the final idea. Things were very positive between them, and they were happy to have everyone as a part of the company. They could align their thoughts and ideas, and they realized that it would be so much fun to work together.

***

Chapter 27

The Promise

The team puts their soul, energy, and passion into a brand for the smile on the customer's face. But when you put together every single smile of every single customer, that's what builds a brand.

Three years, four months later: Billy, Sean, Phil, Dylan, Fia, and surprisingly even Chris, two of his friends, and Smith were all on Chris's boat in Miami, doing the fishing rituals. And to everyone's delight, Twanna also joined them on the boat. Smith, as always, was busy ensuring that everybody got their drinks. It was a delightful moment to see a young and successful team having a great time with their mentor and investor, Chris. One could see the sense of achievement on their faces. They all reflected a positive vibe that shouted, "Life's good! We just need to learn how to live it." Billy wanted to do the same drill he'd done three years ago—fishing, breakfast, snorkeling, trip around the island, and then back to the villa. They caught a lot of small- and medium-sized fish and returned to the villa around 11:00 AM.

Billy was back in Miami to fulfill a promise. He'd once told Chris that he hadn't known how to repay him for all his generosity, but that the day he became successful, he would come back to the same place, and that would be his treat. And that's what they were doing this time. And it wasn't just Billy, but the whole United for a Cause team. They had been successfully running two different brands under the same company, and Chris was an investor in their second brand. Their first brand was purely a tech-support service brand, as none of them had a lot to invest. The brand was an online aggregator that did media buying for all forms of media. They already had their presence all across the United States and now were planning to take it global.

The second brand, where Chris was an investor, created school-level leagues for tennis, table tennis, and golf. They would hunt for talent across the country for all the three sports and put them in the professional circuit. They were also managing talent and executing long-term contracts with them. Both the brands were doing exceedingly well, and even Chris was extremely happy, not because he was an investor, but because of Billy's success.

United for a Cause realized very clearly that whatever they had achieved had a deep connection with Chris, and this trip was to show their respect and gratitude to him. And these were the moments that Chris got a kick out of, motivating him to enable more entrepreneurs. He wouldn't express it, but Billy knew very well how happy he was to see all of them having so much fun in his villa, and somewhere, he was the epicenter.

Billy hadn't been using a crutch or a wheelchair. Last year, he'd surprised Twanna at the airport when she came over to Chicago for some work by going to the airport without any help. Since then, he had been successfully using his artificial limb. His artificial limb not only enabled him to walk properly but also helped him regain his sense of touch and temperature. A technology which had been under development for many years was now a reality. And Billy had been able to almost get back to normal. Three years ago, Billy would have never imagined this life. But he was on a journey where there were no expectations, he gave his best and kept working persistently. The combination of honesty, hard work, and smart work never failed him.

United for a cause, as well as Chris, were a bunch of chain smokers, but they were on their path to reformation. They were now successful non-smokers. They learnt it the hard way, but they believed that it is never too late to change yourself. They were on the path towards responsibility. The very thought of harming themselves was against their journey. So they all made a conscious effort to quit smoking and set examples for others. Chris was even working on a nicotine free campaign.

They reached the villa, asked for some mojitos, and dived into the pool. Billy took it easy and sat inside the pool with Twanna. They had been in touch all these years and were very good friends. She always appreciated Billy's hard work and dedication and was extremely proud and happy to learn so many new things from him. Billy always loved talking to her and stayed in touch with her constantly. Twanna had also come to Chicago twice in between to meet Billy. Every time they met, they cherished their friendship, and Billy always considered himself lucky to have gone to that restaurant for lunch where he'd met her. Billy was so busy with his new business that he never got the time to make new friends. But the reality was that he was happy with his old friends and never felt the need for new friends. Twanna had been a great moral support for him, and this time he convinced her to be with them for all the three days that they stayed in Miami. They just loved talking to each other and never dared to go beyond that. But Billy was very hopeful that maybe one day he would propose to her and they would get married. Billy had his eyes set on her from the moment he'd seen her at the restaurant.

In the meantime, the Graham's were extremely proud of Billy. They were never driven by money, but by kindness and love. They were proud about Billy's vision and where he wanted to be sooner or later. They would not have asked for a better son and felt that even if they were not rich, their unconditional kindness gave them the best gift—their children.

Asha was now a permanent employee at Marque.Inc. She was working as a senior digital marketing strategist. She was also very happy with her job because she'd always wanted to work in this industry where every day was a new challenge. She was planning on getting married this year to her childhood sweetheart. They were an example of true love and made a great couple.

Two years later, United for a Cause sold both their brands at a great valuation and started constructing their orphanage, which they named based on their parent company, United for a Cause. They all were eagerly looking forward for the completion and launch of this project. Five years of consistent hard work, partnership, and a focused drive got them here, and they were nothing but extremely proud of themselves.

Billy finally got the courage and asked Twanna to be his girlfriend. He'd always known she was the one, and a few months into the relationship he proposed. Twanna said yes, and they got a beautiful new house by the lake, where they led their married life. She later volunteered and joined them in their orphanage as a teacher.

Chris, as always, lived a flamboyant life and kept inspiring and mentoring many more people like Billy. He lived up to his core belief of sharing knowledge.

"Dreams do come true, when you work persistently toward making them real. So keep dreaming and you will definitely find a way to fulfill your dreams," said Chris.

***

www.khanindrabarman.com

www.ingramcontent.com/pod-product-compliance
Lightning Source LLC
Chambersburg PA
CBHW020903180526
45163CB00007B/2611